About the Cover

The feather is a composite, a collage depicting the prize we receive when we eat cleaner food.

On the cover, we notice the colors of the seven basic energy centers, located along the spine in the human body.

The red represents our root/base center, (located at the bottom of our spines). The happy pig symbolizes the bottom of the totem pole in terms of foods, meat being very acid.

The cake on the orange regeneration center represents refined grains and sugar. This combination is equally acidic.

Next, we rise to the yellow, solar plexus area in the body. The salmon here begins to become a less toxic food. Although acid, when eaten as 20% of a meal, its protein can be beneficial.

The green is located at our hearts. The apple, although less acid, represents a majority of the fruit we eat, which are acid. Lemons, limes, raw tomatoes and avocados are, however, alkaline producing.

The blue center located at our throats has the symbol of millet. Millet and buckwheat are the only alkaline grains.

The purple center, located between our eyes (at the 3rd eye area) depicts kale, symbolizing all of the dark green leafy vegetables, which are alkaline and therefore beneficial.

The white, located at the top of our heads is symbolic of the grasses. Wheat, kamut and barley grasses are superfoods when they are freshly juiced because they greatly enhance our alkalinity and ability to heal.

Many Alkaline Blessings to you,
Zhena

Alkaline Cuisine

Alkaline Cuisine
*An easy, delicious transitional cookbook for those
who want to boost their health, vitality, and vibrancy*

Published by Narsisus Press
Denver, Colorado

Text and graphics copyright 2010-2013 by Zhéna.
All rights reserved.

ISBN: 978-0-9847373-2-1
1. Cookbook, 2. Health & Fitness, 3. Author, 4. Title

Library of Congress Catalog-in-Publication data is available upon request.

All rights reserved
Printed in the United States of America

No part of this publication can be reproduced, stored in retrieval system, or transmitted in any form or by any means, electronic, mechanical, photocopying, recording, scanning, or otherwise, except as permitted under Section 107 or 108 of the 1976 United States Copyright Act, without either prior written permission of the publisher or the author.

Trademarks: Zhéna, the Zhéna logo, and the Alkaline Feather are trademarks of the author. The Narsisus Press Mark, Narsisus Press, and all other trademarks referred to herein are the intellectual property of LifeColors Production Group, LLC or its affiliates.

Limit of Liability/Disclaimer of Warranty: While the publisher and the author have used their best efforts in preparing this book, they make no representations or warranties to the accuracy and completeness of the contents of this book and specifically disclaim any implied warranties of merchantability or fitness for a particular purpose. No warranty may be created or extended by sales representatives or written sales materials. The advice and strategies contained herein may not be suitable for your situation. You should consult with a professional or a medical practitioner where appropriate. Neither the publisher nor the author shall be liable for any loss of profit or any other commercial damages, including but not limited to special, incidental, consequential, or other damages.

10 9 8 7 6 5 4 3 2 1

Disclaimer

This book is a reference work. It is not intended to treat, diagnose, or prescribe. The information contained herein is in no way to be considered as a substitute for consultation with duly licensed health care professionals.

The information contained in this book is provided as general information. As part of the information presented in this book, the reader understands that this book discusses the concept of Alkaline Cuisine.

The reader agrees to assume acceptable responsibility for any and all risks associated with reading this book and using this method.

The information presented in this book is not intended to represent that the Alkaline Cuisine or any other method is used to diagnose, treat, cure, or prevent any disease or psychological disorder.

The Alkaline Cuisine or any other method is not a substitute for medical or psychological treatment.

Any stories or testimonials presented in this book do not constitute a warranty, guarantee, or prediction regarding the outcome using the Alkaline Cuisine or any other method described herein for any particular issue.

The author and the publisher accept no responsibility or liability whatsoever for the use or misuse of the information contained in this book, including but not limited to explanations of the Alkaline Cuisine methods, training, and related activities.

The author and the publisher strongly advise that the reader seek professional advice as appropriate before making any health decisions.

May all beings, big and small, near and far, human and non-human be Happy, Healthy and Realized

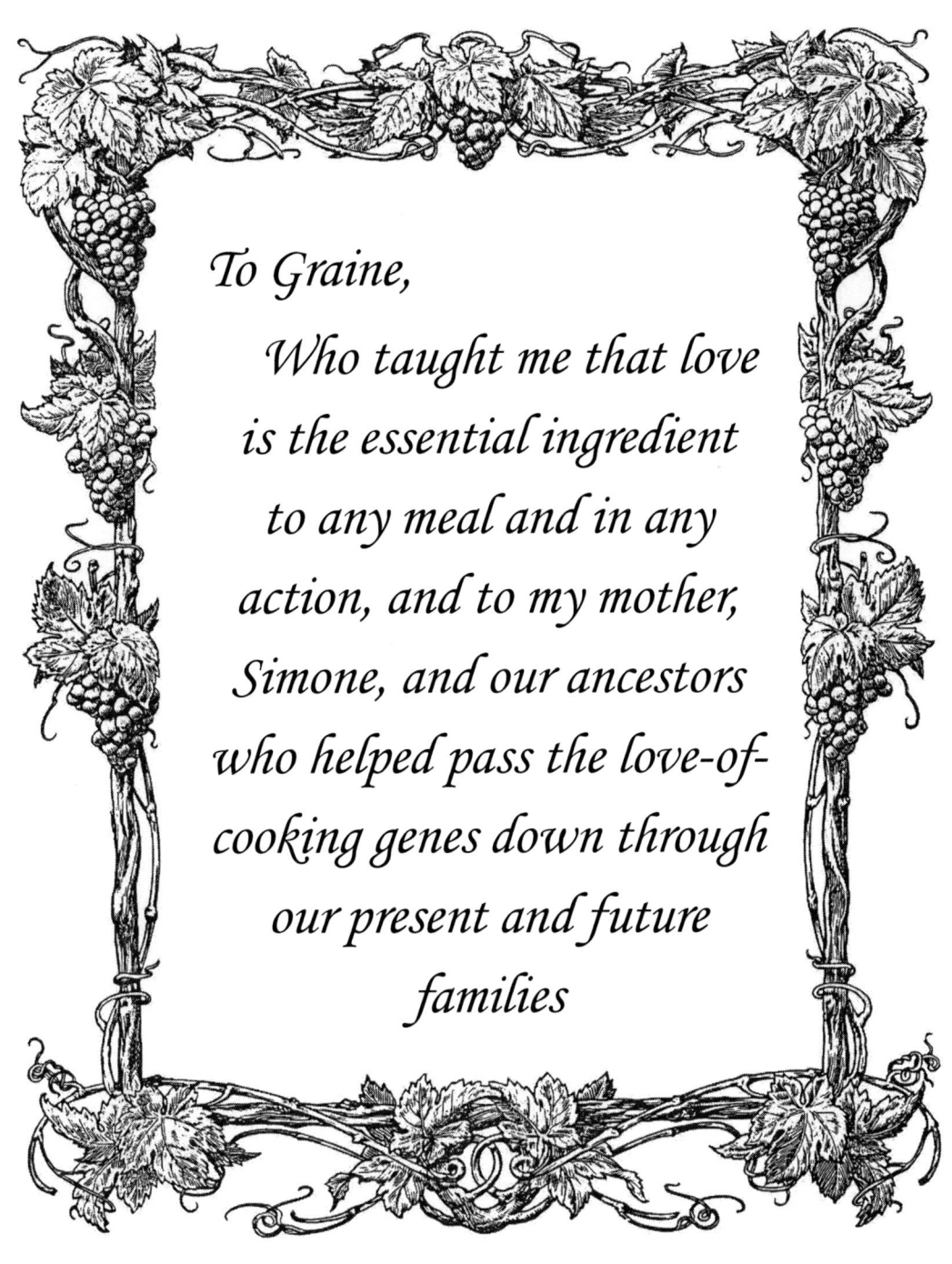

To Graine,

Who taught me that love is the essential ingredient to any meal and in any action, and to my mother, Simone, and our ancestors who helped pass the love-of-cooking genes down through our present and future families

Acknowledgements

Great Mystery, You, whose omnipresence warms my heart, feeds my soul and unites us all, I am grateful for your Blessings

My heartfelt thank-yous go out to:

My Mom and Dad, who many years ago helped me open a natural food bakery, and a restaurant in Amherst, Massachusetts.

Tante Lucile, you opened the door for me to see that when we open our eyes, we can learn what the Creator provides for us in our natural environments…herbs…wild foods…even certain "weeds".

Kathy Pucket, you traded your delicious artwork for conversational French lessons back in the 80s. Your graceful drawings are a gift for all eyes.

Dr. Randall Davis, my Pagosa dentist, bluegrass musician, sculptor, painter, school bus driver and mover of buildings! You made time to draw foods you never heard of for this book. What a special soul you are.

Darling Dominique, it took you oh so many hours working in the cabin to piece together the old and new recipes. I appreciate you, your expertise, your stick-to-itiveness and, most of all, your great, big, sensitive heart.

Sha:nta, you have been with me as I began my vegetarian journey at your conception. You have survived my experiments, failures, and surprises...the non-dairy, the dairy, the raw, the macrobiotic, the Indian, the catering jobs, the herbs, the fasts... You have patiently and most lovingly been my best taster, best sense of humor, and invaluable friend and daughter.

Caroline Foster, thank you for typing and editing the dental chapter. Thank you Dr. Mills for graciously sponsoring Caroline's contribution.

Jackie and the entire Pagosa Springs Library staff, I appreciate you for your time, patience and generous help that went far beyond the call of your job descriptions.

Kelly Evans, the contents of this book stretched your envelope. Thank you for the innumerable hours it has taken you to transform my pebble scratch into a real book!

Thank you Art Line Graphics of Sedona, Arizona for transforming my drawing into a professional and beautiful cover.

Thank you Linda Paris for the contribution of your mighty and conscious athletic evolution.

I appreciate all of you so much. *Zhéna*

Alkaline Cuisine

It can be a huge challenge to be able to feel peaceful or be productive when our bodies hurt. However, we can feel better, rid ourselves of pain and toxins, in order to feel strong and vital. We begin by changing our attention from our "condition" to how we want to feel. Then it's a simple transition, i.e. from eating Russian dressing to enjoying guacamole dressing.

This easy-to-read Cookbook offers help for all, including athletes. It includes four generations of multicultural quick recipes, a getting-started ingredient and herb pantry list and a special chapter on Dental Health. This Cookbook is chock full of recipes and suggestions which are helping so many people to feel better, happier, and more productive.

Table of Contents

Alphabetical List of Recipes	ii
Preface	vii
Introduction	ix
Getting Started	1
Basic Pantry List	10
Herbs and Spices	11
Herbs with Food	15
A Few Food Stories	16
A Real Story...Linda	19
Morning Foods	21
Beverages	28
Appetizers	38
Soups	58
Salads	72
Entrées	91
East Indian	161
Sauces and Condiments	183
Desserts and Breads	190
Addendum	250
Food for Teeth	268
About the Author	302

Alphabetical List of Recipes

A Birthday Cake	249
Addendum	250
Agave-Mustard Sauce	157
Aioli	157
Almost Alexandro's Cactus	108
Alternate Pis à la Dière Crust	52
Amaranth Flour Cookies	255
Appetizers	38
Apple Spice Cake	194
Artichokes	101
Asian Dressing	84
Asian Noodles	123
Asian Tofu	135
Asian Wrap	151
Asparagus (Grilled)	102
Asparagus Bread	195
Avocado Dressing	84
Ayurvedic Cooking	162
Babaganouche Dip	39
Bagels (Craig's French Black Bread)	213
Baked Potato Party	127
Banana Cake (Eggless)	197
Banana Smoothie	31
Banana-Nut Cake	196
Banana-Tofu Pie	198
Basic Pantry List	10
Basic Veggie Soup	59
Basmati Rice	172
Bath Balls (Effervescent)	264
Bean Salad (Classic Cold)	73
Beans (Cooking)	92
Beans (Refied)	103
Beans	93
Beet-Za	104
Beverages	28
Black Bean Soup	60
Bragg Liquid Aminos-Ginger Sauce	157
Bran Muffins	22
Bread	199
Brie and Crackers	40
Buckwheat Pancakes (Eggless)	23
Burdock	166
Cactus (Almost Alexandro's)	108
Canning (fruit)	219
Carob Cake	200
Carob-Mint Brownies	201
Carrot Beet Salad	75
Carrot Cabbage Salad (Fresh)	75
Carrot Cabbage Soup	61
Carrot Cake	202
Carrots & Potatoes (Roasted)	107
Carrot Soup (The Best)	61
Carrots (Tunisian)	106
Cashew-Ginger Sauce	158
Cauliflower Curry	171
Cereal (Hot)	26
Chapatis	168
Chaunce	169
Cheese Fondue	41
Cheese (Yogurt)	57
Cherry Clafoutis	203
Chili Bean Dip	42

Chocolate	204	Drying Foods	253
Chutney (Mango)	186	During the Dental Work	277
Classic Cold Bean Salad	73	Eating Locally	90
Coconut Almond Bars	209	Effervescent Bath Balls	264
Coconut Candies	182	Egg Fu-less Yung	112
Coconut Macaroons-1	210	Egg Rolls	44
Coconut Macaroons-2	211	Egg Substitute (Seeds as)	261
Coconut Macaroons-3 (Eggless)	212	Eggplant (Middle East)	114
Coffee	251	Eggshell Pots	113
Cold Sauce	158	Endives	45
Cole Slaw	76	Entrées	91
Composting	100	Equine Help	265
Cooking Beans	92	Fat Burning	254
Couscous	110	Felafel	115
Crackers	43	Fennel (Fresh)	116
Craig's French Black Bread Bagels	213	Festive Fruit Punch	31
Cranberry Nut Bread	205	Figs (Dried)	217
Cranberry Oat Cookies	206	Food for Teeth	268
Cranberry Oat Flour Cookies	207	French Onion Soup	63
Cranberry Sauce	184	French Wrap	153
Cream Cheese Frosting	208	Fresh Carrot-Cabbage Salad	75
Crêpes	215	Frosting (Cream Cheese)	208
Cucumbers (Stuffed)	76	Frosting (Fruit Glaze)	220
Curried Rice Salad	80	Fruit Canning	219
Dahl: Red Lentil Soup	169	Fruit Crisp	218
Dandelion Salad	77	Fruit Frosting Glaze	220
Date-Nut Bread	216	Fruit Pies	230
Dental Materials: The Best Choices	290	Fruit Salad	78
Desert (The)	252	Fun Foods for Children	267
Desserts and Breads	190	Garam Masala	170
Down-Under Soup	62	Gazpacho	64
Dried Figs	217	Ghee	165
Dried Lima Bean Salad	74	Ginger Dunking Cookies	222
		Gingerbread	221
		Glaze (Fruit Frosting)	220

Gluten Free Cookies	256	Jello-2	225
Gluten Intolerance	255	Kato-Persimmon Bread	229
Gluten-Free Pie Crust	256	Kebobs	121
Gnocchi	119	Kitchari (Mung Beans & Rice)	173
Gomasio	185	Kitchari (Red Lentils & Buckwheat)	174
Grain Burgers	150	Leafy Greens	175
Grain	84	Leeks	121
Granola Pie Crust	223	Lentil Soup	64
Granola	24	Licorice Candy	226
Grape Leaves (Stuffed)	55	Lima Bean Salad (Dried)	74
Green Chili	117	Low Glycemic Foods	258
Green Drink	29	Making Ghee	166
Green Wrap	152	Making Gnocchi	120
Greens	98	Making Pistou	69
Grilled Asparagus	102	Making Salve	266
Guacamole Tostada	118	Making Yogurt	248
Guacamole	46	Mango Chutney	186
Guacamole-Bean Dip	47	Matzo Ball Soup	65
Halavah	181	Mayonnaise	187
Harissa	111	Melon Salad	78
Herb Biscuits / Bread	223	Mexican Rice	122
Herbs and Foods (Properties of)	164	Middle East Eggplant	114
Herbs and Spices (List of)	11	Middle Eastern Wrap	152
Herbs with Foods	15	Mindful Eating	36
Hermits	224	Minestrone Soup	70
Horseradish Sauce	158	Minimum Daily Requirements for Healthy Teeth	279
Hot Cereal	26	Mood Swings	191
Huggins System and Quantum Dental Health System	288	Morning Foods	21
Hummus	48	Muffins	26
Incense	257	Muffins (Pumpkin)	237
Indian Recipes	161	Mung Bean Sprout Salad	79
Italian Dressing	84	Nightshades	259
Italian Wrap	153	Noodles (Asian)	123
Jello-1 (Aspic)	49	Nori Rolls	124

Nut Milks	30	Red Lentil & Buckwheat Kitchari	174
Oatmeal	126	Red Lentil Dahl Soup	67
Oils for Sinuses	260	Rice	96
Olive Quick Bread	227	Rice (Basmati)	172
Pain D'epices (Honey Bread)	228	Rice (Mexican)	122
Pan Fried Tofu	138	Rice (Saffron Sweet)	179
Pancakes (Wholewheat)	27	Rice (Sweet)	180
Pâté	50	Rice Balls	240
Pepitas (Roasted)	53	Rice Pudding-1	241
Peppers (Stuffed)	126	Rice Pudding-2	241
Pico de Gallo	188	Rice Salad (Curried)	80
Pie (Pumpkin)	238	Ricotta Cheese Cake	242
Pie Crust	231	Roasted Carrots & Potatoes	107
Pie Crust (Easy)	232	Roasted Pepitas	53
Pie Crust (Granola)	233	Russian Dressing	85
Pineapple Upside-Down Cake	234	Sabzi: String Beans	177
Pis à la Dière	51	Saffron Sweet Rice	179
Pis à la Dière Crust (Alternate)	52	Salad Dressings	84
Pistou	69	Salads	72
Pizza Dough	105	Salmon	130
Poppyseed Cake	235	Salmon-2	131
Potato Leek Soup	68	Salmon in Rice Wrappers	54
Potato Salad	79	Salve (To Make)	266
Pretty Good Tofu	143	Satiation	88
Protein Bars (Wolfberry)	247	Sauce (Thick)	146
Protein Drink	30	Sauces and Condiments	183
Prune Tart	236	Sauces for Veggies	157
Pumpkin Muffins	237	Seeds as an Egg Substitute	261
Pumpkin Pies	238	Sesame Dressing	85
Quatres Quarts	239	Setting the Mood	37
Quiche	128	Shepherd's Pie	132
Quick Bread (Olive)	227	Shredded Wrap	152
Quick Green Veggies	179	Sorbet	243
Ratatouille	129	Soup au Pistou	69
Recipe for Healthy Teeth	278	Soup for Couscous	111

Soups	58	Tofu Lasagna	137
Spanish Wrap	153	Tofu Mayonnaise	85
Spinach Velouté	68	Tofu Salad	139
Split Pea Soup	66	Tofu Sesame Sauce	159
Sprouted Salad	81	Tofu Spinach Walnut Loaf	143
Squash Puff	133	Tofu Spread	141
Steamed Wrap	152	Tofu Stuffed Romas	144
String Beans	134	Tomato Salad Provençal	83
String Beans (Sabzi)	177	Tossed Salad (Variations)	86
Stuffing with Tofu	141	Tostada (Guacamole)	118
Sun Tea	33	Tunisian Carrots	106
Sweet and Sour Sauce	159	TVP Burgers	149
Sweet Rice	180	Vegetable Broth	66
Sweeteners (List of)	192	Vegetable Fried Rice	147
Tabouleh	82	Vegetable Rice Casserole	148
Tahini	189	Vegetable Soup-2	71
Tahini Candies	244	Vegetable Soup-2	71
Tahini Cookies	244	Veggie Burgers	149
Tartar	56	Veggie Soup (Basic)	59
Tea (Sun)	33	Veggie Stew	178
Tea (Yogi)	167	Veggies (Quick Green)	176
Teas	32	Vulcan Wedding Cake	246
Thick Sauce	146	Wheat Grass Juice	34
Tofu	135	Whole Wheat Pancakes	27
Tofu (Asian)	135	Wok Cooking	145
Tofu (Pan Fried)	138	Wolfberry Protein Bars	247
Tofu (Pretty Good)	143	Wood Stove Cooking	262
Tofu and Rice	137	Wraps	151
Tofu Burgers-1	136	Yams (Baked)	154
Tofu Burgers-2	149	Yogi Tea	167
Tofu Crustless Pie	142	Yogurt (Making)	248
Tofu in Cold Salads	140	Yogurt Beverage	35
Tofu in Soups	140	Yogurt Cheese	57
Tofu Kabobs	136	Zucchini (Baked)	155
		Zucchini (Shredded)	156

Preface

Oh yes, Graine is coming...Not only are we to have another baby, but Graine is coming all the way from France to help us out. This means time together, time making special yummies in the kitchen...smelling the raspberries cooking down into jam...weighing out the eggs and flour on the scale...and waiting "forever" for those "krepfuns" to rise...finally even a small taste covered our noses with powdered sugar, then we bit into those jelly doughnuts. And that is how it began...watching and helping my French Grand-mother in the kitchen.

Since those days, back in Pelham, N.Y., those days of dunking sugar cubes into her coffee after dinner, (she'd call them "ducks!"), the meats and sauces, pork drippings on toast with salt, sugar, cream, white flour and chocolate have all been put to rest.

Then there was Gramps and Florie...who would have their own favorites for us...the "Shnekins" from the N.Y.C. bakery, were a treat because Gramps and I would walk there arm in arm, he always on the outside to protect me... Although the home cooked meals of tongue and canned asparagus left my stomach and brain in bedlam, what could a Jewish Grandmother do, but to offer her best!

What came through on both sides of the Grand-family was lots of love and good intentions.

Today the meats, sugars, dairy, canned and frozen foods are only a memory. After having metamorphosed through the yogurt and salad stage which left me a bit healthier and with more energy but soon, very cold and spacey; so the search ensued.

What came next was to "cook" food. Cooking food for a long time got the energy out and into us. And so began the macrobiotic, non-dairy phase. Some pounds came off, and I felt stronger, but I also became so rigid that I could hardly stand myself, much less others.

Finally, I came across the idea of eating within the laws of nature. I saw that there were reasons to choose particular foods depending on our body's constitution, the environment we lived in, and whatever ailments we were trying to heal. All clean foods are good for some people, under certain circumstances. Local foods are for the most part better than foreign imported foods, but because of our sometimes unnatural lifestyles, it was to our advantage to include some healthy foods from other parts of the globe.

It is my hope that these recipes will help you grow physically, mentally, and emotionally. I trust that you will find the inner or outer Guidance to help you choose what foods help you to be grounded, centered, and full of vital energy.

Some of the recipes come from my non-dairy days, some from the French days, some from the Ayurvedic ways, and some from the present alkaline times.

Introduction

So much has happened in the past two decades, since first offering part of this revised cookbook to cooking class participants. Sha:nta, my chief taste tester-daughter and I have moved from Shelburne Falls, MA to Colorado. She has since finished high school, college and has moved to New York City.

My older daughter, Dominique, has moved from the east to the west coast and is now temporarily here in Pagosa. She cooks all of the meals for her dog Nikki; meals that if she were not a vegetarian, she could eat as well. Her dog, Nikki, is an eight year old Pit mix who had lots of digestive problems with store bought food. Nikki is now happy and healthy with home cooking and raw food.

Each time we moved, we delighted in new foods and unique preparations. So, in twenty years, having gone through several spiritual ventures, each with its food specialties, it was time to revise and add to the original cookbook, making it a transitional guide for healthier eating.

The original cookbook left off with some Ayurvedic recipes from India. The way herbs and spices are included in these dishes makes it a very digestible and tasty culinary venture. Revising the old recipes has meant changing over from honey to agave, which is less glycemic. Bragg Liquid Aminos has replaced Tamari, because it is not fermented. Yeast goodies have been omitted and replaced by quick or sprouted grain options. Food combining and acid-alkaline balancing have taken a priority in the addition of recipes for health reasons.

My friend Eagle told me that I should write a book about Coyote romping through the garden. Coyote is not only a trickster, but the one who brings the darkness to the light so that the darkness can be transmuted. In North Dakota the "garden" means "your life". If you are asked, "How's ya garden?" when it is 30 degrees below zero, you can talk about your family, friends, business, etc…

Here in Pagosa, when I inquired at the local City Market, "Which fruit and vegetables are not genetically engineered?" I was told "None, all the produce has been engineered." I call this coyote stomping through our garden.

The Ayurveds say that the best food we can eat is cooked by our self, the next best is cooked by our mother and the next best is cooked by our beloved. All of the processed, packaged, trucked, chemicalized, hormone, preservative, colored, sugar, quick comfort foods are obviously not included in this Ayurvedic strategy. When we eat dead processed food, how can we wake up physically or spiritually?

How can we rise above survival mentality? Eating dead processed food helps us remain asleep. Eventually our bodies will become tired and sick. We won't have the energy to think outside the box nor will we have the stamina to make the extra effort to go beyond pillaging and polluting thoughts and actions. The closer we eat to the garden – i.e. fresh veggies, the more energy our bodies will have for clearer thinking, vitality, creativity, cooperation, sports, fun and the pursuit of truth.

My intention for this cookbook is to offer more than recipes, i.e. to teach you how to cook, eat and feel better. It IS possible to transition. Enjoying a cheeseburger can develop into enjoying and benefiting from eating a homemade veggie burger and sprouted grains.

This book offers you ways to evolve from having a lethargic, acid body to an alkaline, energetic more conscious lifestyle.

I am excited to share what I've learned with you.

Dear Friends,

Some of the recipes in this book will have a small feather with a number on it to help you determine the acid-alkaline value of the food. Any recipe of 4 or below is acid and will not have a feather.

If a recipe calls for ghee or Bragg Liquid Aminos it will be more acid than if you use olive oil or omit the Bragg.

This legend gives you an approximate notion of the acid-alkaline level in the food. The goal is to eat 80% Alkaline– 20% acid.

- 7 Greens
- 6 Cooked Greens
- 5 Grains & Beans
- 4 Fish
- 3 Fruit
- 2 Sugar
- 1 Meat

Getting Started

Let's begin to understand how improving our diet can help us feel better. This can have a rippling effect to help our families, co-workers and beyond. Let us explore the ancient art of food combining, and then move to acid-alkaline foods.

Part of food combining for vegetarians is making sure that meals include a complete protein; that is beans and rice, pasta and cheese. Another aspect of food combining has to do with digestion. Digested food is food that is broken down which can be assimilated by the body so that the food's nutrients can be utilized.

When food combination is not proper, then the food putrefies, rots, or ferments in the body. This can cause gas, body odor, malnutrition, Candida, fungus, headaches, aches and pains, and a host of diseases.

When a protein (meat-fish-beans) is mixed with fruit, i.e. jam, catsup, or sugary sauces, the protein putrefies. The rotting food cannot be absorbed as a nutrient and it becomes toxic. The body has a natural tendency to buffer these toxins. It creates cholesterol, thus, a way to lower cholesterol to eat foods that are non-toxic. Some toxic foods include processed foods, and preservatives.

Another food combination that hurts people is mixing grains with sugar which can cause a yeast overgrowth. Many people already have Candida. This can arise from taking antibiotics and not replenishing the gut's beneficial bacteria with acidophilus. Yeast overgrowth can come from a compromised immune system, which can come from breathing toxic air, having amalgam fillings, having heavy metals in the blood and organs or from injections containing aluminum, eating canned food, or from mercury contaminated fish. Eating grains with sugar (toast and jam, cereal and fruit) can add to the Candida (yeast overgrowth) problem.

If your body has an overgrowth of yeast, (you probably have

gas, headaches, yeast infections, or severe bloating). The sugar and carbs feed the yeast overgrowth, as does any fermented food or drink. Fermentation is not digestion. Candida can develop into fungus, which can get worse.

After a meal, do you crave a sweet?

That's Candida, which wants to be fed! So, it is best not to eat protein and sugars together and do not eat fermented/fungus foods (tempeh, wine, beer, yeasted bread, vinegar, catsup, mushrooms, tamari, moldy cheeses (blue) if you want to reverse your discomfort and develop vitality.

DO:
- Eat fruit alone. If you are going to eat fruit dark, local, in season berries are a good choice for their antioxidant properties.
- Eat lots of green veggies: raw and some steamed. (The raw veggies provide enzymes which help your body to digest food.)
- Eat protein with greens, i.e. salmon and salad and broccoli.
- Eat grains and greens together: rice and steamed veggies not protein and grains or protein and sugar (i.e. meat and catsup).
- Eat protein and greens at one meal (tofu and salad).

Live Blood Cell Analysis has become a way to test for yeast, fungus, heavy metals, and a clogged immune system. Dr. Robert Young was my teacher more than a decade ago. He stressed the importance of acid-alkaline balance in the body. It's quite simple. When our blood is acid, we grow towards disease. When we are alkaline, we've given our bodies the building blocks to heal themselves.

Here's the ratio and how to achieve the ratio.

If you are relatively healthy, eat 80% alkaline and 20% acid. An easy way to grasp this is to have a small portion (20%) of acid on your plate and lots of alkaline (80%) food.

If you are wondering what is acid and what is alkaline, this too is simple: there are a few fruits which are alkaline: lemons, limes, avocados, and FRESH tomatoes. (It's the final stage of the digested lemons and limes, the ash, which makes them alkaline.)

ALL other fruit are acid. This does not mean never to eat them. They become part of the 20% acid portion in the diet. Fresh, uncooked vegetables are alkaline.

All sprouts, sprouted grains and beans are alkaline. Soaked nuts and seeds (almonds, filberts, pecans, walnuts, pumpkin, and sunflower seeds) are alkaline.

There are two grains that are alkaline, millet and buckwheat. All other grains are acid (unless sprouted).

All meat and fish are acid, as is sugar.

Let's talk about meat and fish.

The cleanest meat you can get is venison. People often ask, "What about free range eggs, chicken and turkey?" Here's the glitch. Yes, free range anything is better than imprisoned hormone laden animal meat. Yes, there are grass fed open range ranches that offer high quality meat.

The problem arises when animals are fed corn. Corn is in most 'feed'. Corn contains a multitude of fungi. When people eat fungus foods (like the black fungus in some Chinese dishes, and corn fed animals,) the tendency is to become infested with fungus.

(People with fungus under their toe nails know how difficult it is to clear that out. The reason is because the fungus is systemic and is just presenting itself on the outside of the body.)

If you are going to eat meat, make sure it's in small portions. Eat meat with some fresh salad so that the salad's enzymes digest the protein.

Now for the fish.

The biggest concern here is the possibility of mercury in fish. You also don't want to eat fish that are farm raised until you know if the ingredients in the pellets that these fish are fed are healthy. Do they contain hormones to fatten them up? You also want to know that the waters the fish are caught in are clean.

You do NOT want to eat fish that eat scum. These are bottom feeders, including catfish and shellfish. You do want to choose fish like wild Alaskan salmon, or clean river water (if that's possible) trout. Talk to the suppliers who provide fish to your local grocer to find out where the fish has been caught.

If you choose to make changes in your life in order to be healthier, please examine your cooking containers. If your pots and pans are made of aluminum or have a Teflon type coating, throw them out. They contaminate food with heavy metal and possible carcinogens. Use enamel or glass. Use stainless steel if you don't scour it. (Scouring stainless causes particles of the metal to dislodge into the food.)

A word about super foods.

Wheat grass and barley grass are fabulous because they are alkaline and they detox the body. As always, fresh is best, but powders come in handy when traveling.

Spirulina and chlorella are algae so they feed fungus, so you're not going to want to eat these no matter what the other claims for health may be.

Peanuts and corn are highly toxic foods because of the multitude of fungus they contain. It's best never to eat them. Eating almond or sesame butter will provide some calcium. These butters are so much cleaner, microbially speaking, than peanut butter.

Fruits and vegetables.

Eat organic fruits and vegetables that are locally grown, which are in season. Sometimes you will choose ones that have traveled long distances. Ask if alar has been used on apples, or have the citrus been radiated or the bananas gassed. In any case choose firm undamaged produce, free from dried edges or brown spots. You can rinse fruit and vegetables in a vegetable cleaner and water to remove external sprays.

Some of you may be athletes and may be drinking protein powders and sucking down glucose. There IS a healthier route. If, for instance you are a biker, try eating dates, raw beet slices, and soaked almonds. Take a 'green drink' on your ride. For the dinner before your event, eat some quinoa. After your ride, drink some fresh wheat grass juice to help with the lactic acid build up.

Let's talk about dairy.

Dairy is acid and tends to clog the immune system. However, the Ayurvedic tradition is big on dairy. So, here's what I suggest: eliminate dairy from your diet if you have allergies such as a stuffy nose, sore throat, or other congestion.

If you are going to eat dairy, try goat milk products and add cinnamon, cardamom, and clove powder if the dairy is in yogurt or milk form. Consume dairy when you can be active and when the weather is warm. This will help you to metabolize it.

By now, if you are used to the S.A.D. (standard American diet) you must be wondering, "What should I eat?" This will sound absurd at first, but you will feel so much better if you eat the same way for breakfast, lunch and supper. Eat green, green, green!

For breakfast, instead of starting the day with a mountain of acidity (o.j., toast, eggs, hash browns, or sugary commercial cereal) start off with a fresh green drink, soaked almonds, and veggie soup or a salad, or cooked buckwheat or millet.

For lunch eat a green salad with soaked pumpkin seeds (you can bring them in a baggie to work for your restaurant salad) and a piece of salmon with lemon. Or eat a sprouted grain tortilla roll-up with avocado and veggies.

For supper have some quinoa with fresh string beans, garlic lemon and olive oil and a green salad. You'll awaken the next morning more alert with more and clearer energy for the oncoming day.

If it's a cold winter morning eat some hot cooked millet or buckwheat with cinnamon and soaked nuts.

At the beginning of your change of diet there's a period when you may detox. It depends on what your physical condition was before you started the change. Here especially, lots of fresh green juice and alkaline water will assist in flushing out toxins.

Aim to increase alkaline water consumption to a gallon of water per day. A negative ionizer, in my opinion, provides the best water available for most people. Fill your glass (not plastic) and water bottles with it. This "gallon" is not hard and fast for everyone. Take into consideration your height, weight, area that you live in, health condition, age and activities.

The more you hydrate (gradually), the more your cells can let go of toxins, the better you will feel. Some people drink 2 gallons per day. Your kidneys need time to adjust to the change. Paying attention to your body urine color and pH will be your best guides. Use pH paper to test your saliva or urine.

A short word about salt.

Stop using white table salt. Use pink "real salt" which is full of minerals. Balance, as always is the key to using salt. You will need less real salt than regular table salt.

Experiment with programming your food and beverages. To do this hold your hands around your plate, bowl, glass or cup. Be thankful to all those who have been involved in bringing you this nourishment. These could include the Creator Spirit, the microbes that work in the soil, the devas, the plant spirits, the farmers, the truck drivers, the grocery store cashier and the person who prepared the food for you.

Put your intention into the food, perhaps to clear all toxins and imbalances, then ask that the food rejuvenate you.

Eating Out.

It's helpful to carry a small bottle of cold pressed olive oil, a lemon or lime and some soaked nuts or seeds with you. Many restaurants have a 'salad oil' but it's often kept in a warm place and is low grade. (Heat causes oil to go rancid, to become a carcinogen.) If you order a salad and you add all your fixings you can be social and healthy.

For supper many restaurants can grill fish or veggies. Along with a salad or dinner portion of the side vegetables you'll be fine.

Herb tea or warm water with fresh lemon are preferred alternatives to acid coffee. Sparkling water, Perrier with a twist of lemon or lime can include you in the cocktail portion of socializing. Of course, if you are blessed to live in a place where you have raw food or vegetarian restaurants, they can be fun for your palate, and give you creative ideas for home eating.

For the person who doesn't know how to cook... and would like to learn

A first step in learning how to cook is to start out by using prepared mixes. There are plenty of packaged health foods that only require a few added ingredients. Learn the consistency of cakes, muffins, rice dishes etc...Read the ingredients. Then try to make them from scratch. See what you like or don't care for and substitute your own preferred spices.

Once you learn HOW to cook, you'll be free to create your own flavorful appetizers, entrées, soups, greens, grains, desserts, and beverages. (Of course the simplest and healthiest way to eat is raw.)

Please Note:
T. = Tablespoon
t. = Teaspoon
c. = Cup

You will find recipes marked with an asterisk (*) in this book. Look for them by name in the Alphabetical List of Recipes on page ii at the front of the book.

Basic Pantry List

- Fresh ginger root
- Toasted sesame oil
- Whole cloves and clove powder
- Cold pressed olive oil
- Unsulphered powdered ginger
- Real salt (pink or Himalayan salt)
- Red lentils
- Anise powder
- Green/brown lentils
- Cayenne pepper
- Black beans, dried
- Whole peppercorns
- Basmati rice (from India)
- Turmeric powder
- Fresh lemons/limes
- Cumin powder
- Onions
- Cinnamon sticks
- Garlic (fresh)
- Cinnamon powder
- Molasses
- Cardamom pods
- Agave (dark has more flavor)
- Coriander seeds and powder
- Whole wheat pastry flour
- Peppermint essential oil
- Non-aluminum baking powder
- Vanilla
- Whole peppercorns
- Bragg Liquid Aminos Liquid Amino Acids

Herbs and Spices

When possible, purchase whole herbs to grind in an electric coffee mill as you need them. The flavor will be worth your effort! My friend Stephanie has requested a list of herbs and spices with suggestions for their use. Here's a partial list that could help you get started enhancing the flavors of your concoctions.

Anise: has a strong licorice taste, use fresh 'leaves' on salads, using dry 'leaves' as a tea. The powder is good on cooked carrots

Asafoetida (Hing): has an onion-garlic taste and is used sparingly in curries. It is said to cleanse the colon

Basil: fresh leaves are used to make pesto. These leaves are good in salads and on steamed veggies, pasta and rice. Dried basil is good in veggie soups, along with thyme

Bay leaves: used in veggie soups and with barley or yiyi ren

Burdock: cleaned roots can be added to soups. It has an earthy taste and is grounding

Carob: the powder can be used in hot nut milk drinks instead of cocoa powder with cardamom. (This is a yummy alternative to hot chocolate)

Cardamom: is good in curries, yogurt, sweet rice, apple desserts

Caraway: best with cabbage and to top home-made crackers

Catnip: use dry herb in a tea, or for your minou (kitty)

Cayenne: hot red pepper powder, use sparingly in veggie soups and guacamole. It is said that it helps with circulation

Chervil: use with parsley, thyme and basil, just before serving in soups and carrots

Chives: use finely chopped greens on salads and on all cooked veggies, just before serving. Add to yogurt with some dill, salt, and pepper for a dip. The purple flowers can be eaten in salads

Chili: there are many degrees of heat and a variety of ways to prepare chili. For instance, chipotle is smoked chili. Use in bean dishes or sprinkle it on top of guacamole or mix it in with rice

Cilantro: is the fresh leaf of the coriander seed. This herb is also called Chinese parsley. The fresh leaves can be used to make pesto. Sprinkle the leaves on any veggie, rice noodles, or on top of bean soups, just before serving. Use it in salads, salsa and spring rolls. It's the best food for chelating heavy metals from the body

Cinnamon: use cinnamon sticks as part of making Yogi Tea, or whole in curries or rice. Use the powder with apples, oatmeal, yogurt, carrots, yams, pumpkin, and beets

Coriander: use seeds as a tea or the seed powder in yogurt, curries or rice

Cumin: do not use this if you are on blood thinners. Cumin is a wonderful addition to curries, black beans, red and brown lentils and rice

Curry: actually, curry is a blend of several spices. You roast cinnamon sticks, cumin seed, coriander and cardamom seeds, then powder them adding powered ginger and turmeric, then salt, garlic, black pepper, fenugreek and bay leaf. Curry is used with coconut for curries, (vegetable, red lentil, potato, cauliflower, chickpea, rice, and eggplant)

Dill: use the fresh fern-like leaves with yogurt, in salad dressings, with fish and on cucumbers

Garlic: use minced on any veggie with olive oil: asparagus, artichokes, kale, string beans. Use when cooking fish, soups, rice, pasta, and in salad dressings. This is one of the healthiest foods you can ingest

Ginger: fresh ginger root can be simmered as a tea. 1/2 C of the powder can be put into a hot bath for detox. Use ginger in curries, when baking fish, with yams, carrots, pumpkin, cookies, cakes, and fruit pies

Green onions: use in tabouleh, just before serving on veggies, baked on fish, on salads, rice, pasta, and in wraps

Lavender: use flowers on salads and as tea

Lemon: use the fresh juice on fish, veggies, rice, as a last minute addition to curries, in a fresh glass of water, warm as a tea, in salad dressing. Use the grated rind in cookies and granola bars

Marjoram: use small amounts in salad dressing, on fish, veggies, carrots, potatoes, and tomatoes

Mint: use fresh in salads, spring rolls, tabouleh, and in ice tea. Dry it for tea. Peppermint tea is used for stomach upsets. The essential oil is used topically in a first aid kit for injuries

Mustard: mix mustard powder with water for hot mustard. Dry roast the seeds in a cast iron skillet, to put in kitchari and curries, veggie soups, and basmati rice

Nasturtium: flowers have a peppery taste to enhance fresh salads.

Nutmeg: use grated with apples, pears, fruit pies, on winter squash and rice and pumpkin

Onion: when they sprout, cut the greens for salads and veggies. Use onions in stir fries, steamed veggies, with grains, soups, and French onion pie. Use dehydrated onion on top of string beans, tomatoes, pasta and in salad dressing

Oregano: use when you want that 'Italian' flavor, especially with basil and thyme. Use on tomatoes, bell peppers, in grain stuffing, or steamed artichoke hearts

Parsley: use as the main ingredient in tabouleh. Juice it. Use on salads and in salad dressings, on veggies, in rice, on fresh potatoes and pasta

Piñon: a few piñon nuts flavor home-made crackers, quick breads, salads, steamed greens, grains and hot cereal, and pesto

Pepper: use only freshly ground black or multi-colored peppercorns. Black peppercorns are used in yogi tea. Use in soups, on pasta, on veggies, on grains, especially tasty with quinoa and buckwheat

Poppy seeds: use as a topping on home-made crackers or in quick breads and cakes

Rosemary: you can usually keep a fresh indoor plant growing year-round. Use only the spiky 'leaves' not the stalk to make tea. Use on salads, salad dressings, fish, kale, in soups, on baked potatoes, roasted carrots and potatoes. You can also ingest the orchid-like flowers it makes. Rosemary in grain stuffing is delicious

Saffron: make a tea, or use in rice or on fish

Sage (culinary): make a soothing tea with sage. Use it on baked fish, salads and in wraps. It is also a flavorful last minute addition to rice and soups

Sesame seeds: grind and sprinkle them on top of salads or in wraps. Use these to top home-made crackers. Use in granola bars, and on top of steamed veggies and or grains. These are a good source of calcium

Shallots: have an onion—garlic taste. Use with tofu, steamed greens, grains, stuffing

Thyme: make a tea with it. Use in veggie burgers, Italian dishes, on home-made crackers, in salad dressing on salads, on fish and in rice

Turmeric: volumes could be written about this root, its antibiotic properties, how it can help with diabetes and lung ailments. It is a main ingredient in curry. Small amounts of the powder turn simmering rice into brilliant yellow gold.

Herbs with Foods

Dried beans: garlic, onions, parsley, sage, cilantro, thyme, oregano (bay with lima beans) cumin with black beans

Lentils: cumin, curry with red lentils and coconut

Fresh string beans: garlic, onion, green onion, parsley, lemon juice (at serving time) rosemary, thyme, basil, oregano

Broccoli: basil thyme, rosemary, garlic, onions, lemon, top with dehydrated onions just before serving

Cabbage: onion, garlic, fennel, caraway, Bragg Liquid Aminos, ginger, star anise

Carrots: anise, basil, onions, garlic, shallots, cinnamon, cardamom, clove, parsley, ginger, rosemary, fennel, chives

Fish: anise, garlic, onions, ginger, sage, fennel, Bragg Liquid Aminos, rosemary, thyme

Apples: cinnamon, nutmeg, ginger, cardamom

Pears: clove, nutmeg, ginger, cinnamon, cardamom, lavender flowers

Peaches: ginger, cinnamon

Apricots: cardamom

Grains: onions, garlic, chili, curry, rosemary, parsley, cilantro, saffron, cayenne, pepper, mint in cold salads, sage

Squash (Acorn, Blue Hubbard, etc.): Cinnamon, nutmeg, clove, cardamom, garlic, onions, rosemary, sage, and thyme

Quick breads: onion, garlic, leeks, dill, thyme, rosemary, basil, sage oregano, cinnamon, ginger, nutmeg, clove, cardamom, lemon rind

Pies (fruit): cinnamon, cardamom, raisins, cloves, ginger, lemon peel

Steamed veggies: olive oil, garlic, lemon juice, rosemary, thyme, sage, and oregano

A Few Food Stories

I hope that my sister Diane will forgive me for including our dad's report on her cooking. She, however, wasn't the only one who created almost-inedibles. In junior high school, I was so excited when my parents first left me at home to babysit my younger siblings. I ran straight for the kitchen to make us a treat, fudge. Although I'd never tasted fudge, what I'd seen looked delectable.

Not realizing that recipes for candy needed to be followed closely when peanuts were called for, we got the can out and washed them. I'm not sure why I added food coloring, but what we ended up with was an all-too-sweet-blue-green-thick-goop that none of us kids could eat. No one dared tell our parents how we had wasted the food.

On to my sister's cuisine.

Our dad went to France to visit her. She was so proud to provide him, in the blistering cold, with a hot meal and his favorite dessert. She had prepared stuffed cabbage. Dad's eyes rolled when he related the experience, not wanting to appear unappreciative.

Diane had bought a beautiful large green cabbage. She removed the center and stuffed it with hamburger and baked it! (stuffed cabbage.) Dad ate it. (Actually I recently found a similar recipe with chestnut paste stuffed in between the leaves!)

Then she brought out the coffee cake. Dad was Jewish, so coffee cake to him meant a yeasted morning bread. Diane had found a recipe for the dessert-type coffee cake. When it called for 3 T of coffee, she dipped into the morning brew's container and scooped in the grounds! Crunch! Oops!

I had a shocker at a beautiful restaurant in Vail, Co. My new husband and I returned from the salad bar. The waiter placed my grilled veggies in front of me and I gasped. When he looked at me after serving my husband, he said the usual, "Is everything all right?" I said, "NO, you forgot to cook his salmon." Politely he looked to Mouge and said, "Sir, shall I cook this?" They laughed as it went back to the kitchen.

This is the last story. Ten years ago, here in Pagosa, I went to a new friend's for tea, with a few other neighbors. Her baby sitter arrived with her three year old daughter. She reported to my friend, "She didn't have a big appetite for lunch but ate some celery and a few gold fish".

Immediately I flashed back on the craze when I was young, to eat live gold fish in a telephone booth. (I never did). My friend saw the aghast look on my face and kindly said, "Zhéna, goldfish are a kind of cracker!" How embarrassing not to have known!

Oh, one more story.

It is my good fortune to have a friend. Her name is Naziia. We met in Springfield, MA. She is a beautiful African-American woman and very special.

One day, when she was having dinner at my house, I asked her to put olive oil and lemon on the salad. Surprised, I asked her WHAT she was doing. She calmly explained that this is what her ancestors did…as she rolled the lemon, crushing it on the floor with her bare foot. The zest in the kitchen was wonderful. When she sliced the lemon in two there was so much juice!

Naziia's and our feet will benefit from the lemon oil.

...and another story

In my early 20s, one summer in southern France I was joyfully wrangled to help prepare and sell food at the weekend fête (festival). My job was to make pesto.

As I began peeling garlic, I noticed the older men huddling and laughing. I finally spoke up asking "what was so funny?" "You are peeling the garlic," he said. "Yes, so I can make your pesto." Silence…as I continued peeling. More snickering. "So what is the problem?"

You know how old people are with their wisdom when they approach a young know-it-all? Here I was volunteering to help THEM make money and THEY were laughing at me!

One frumpy older guy turned his head my way and said, "You don't peel garlic." I replied, "I have to." He said, "No." I said, "What are you talking about?" They all laughed.

He said, "Appuis sur la goose d'ail." (Lean on the clove of garlic.) "What???" "With the heel of your hand." "Oh. Okay." "Ouch." "Now what?" "Now the skin falls off without using a knife.!!!"

My brother, James, puts his weight on the side of a knife on top of the clove of garlic to achieve the same result. Once the skin falls away, make checkerboard slits in the clove. Then slice it so that it is finely chopped.

Bon appétit!

A real story...Linda

I suppose in many ways I have been athletic most of my life but I really started when I met my husband in 1985 and he was participating in triathlons. It was shortly after that I also began "training" and have never really stopped. I've done many running races, road and mountain triathlons and a variety of endurance events including an extreme mountain triathlon, 24 hour adventure race and the Death Ride—a 228 mile road bike ride among friends in the mountains of Southwest Colorado.

I've always considered myself healthy and my diet over the years has been an evolution. I've been a vegetarian of some sort since my early 20's. It started with excluding red meat from my diet and over the years has become more strict, vegan and alkaline since my first meeting with Zhéna in 2003.

A couple of years prior I had a digestive analysis done which revealed that I had candida. I made some modifications to my diet and was prescribed some different things by a naturopathic doctor. I never had any "symptoms" so I was told not to worry about it.

I WAS worried and kept searching for an answer, which led me to Zhéna and "live blood analysis". In short...my diet became sugarless, yeast free and more alkaline and I finally became free of candida.

My athletic pursuits struggled during this period, especially with the mind set that you have to continually fuel with sugar during endurance training and racing. While this is true, I found many alternatives to processed sugar. I switched from energy drinks to beet/carrot/celery juices on my long bike rides and dates during my long runs.

I began to notice that I felt really good even after several hours of training. Gone was the nose dripping and phlegm and my breathing became slow and steady. I felt as though I had so much more oxygen!

I did many races over the next few years, but completing the Death

Ride for two consecutive years (2004/2005) is probably the most memorable due to the "low key" nature of the event, the difficulty and the sheer beauty. The ride is 228 miles with 20K elevation. It starts and ends in Durango via the San Juan Skyway.

The first year, 2004, I don't even remember how or why I decided to try this other than a casual invitation from a friend. This is not a ride that attracts a crowd, so when we started with our group of six, I was afraid to tell them that the longest ride I had ever done was 70 miles.

I asked my husband, Keith, if he would drive our support vehicle and planned out what I was going to drink and eat for a 16 hour bike ride. I packed the cooler with several juices, portioned out small bags of dates and raw soaked almonds, and filled small containers with brown rice and quinoa.

I felt great and finished the ride much to my surprise! I had no intention to do it again until the same friend said, "but we're going to ride the loop in a clockwise direction" which in 25 years had never been tried.

I guess he got me going, because I decided to do it again the next year in 2005. The extra challenge here was that most of the really hard climbing came after 150 miles of riding. If it wasn't hard enough, that year for part of the ride we had rain, wind and some pretty dangerous conditions. We started with nine riders and eight of us finished.

My food and drink routine was more or less the same as the previous year and I remember one of the guys commenting that he was amazed anyone could do a ride like that eating "rabbit food".

I maintain a consciousness about proper diet. It takes time, planning and discipline but I would recommend it to anyone who is serious about health and fitness. I feel good about what goes into my body and most of the friends that I work out with are at least ten years younger than I at age 48.

Zhéna has been an incredible guide along this path with her wealth of knowledge about food and nutrition.

Morning Foods

A cup of warm water with fresh lemon juice will start your day with a mini-cleanse

Most of the following recipes are for transitioning. The healthiest way to begin the day, from an alkaline point of view, is to make a green juice and eat soaked nuts or seeds, or cooked millet, or buckwheat, or a tossed salad with soaked nuts & seeds.

Bran Muffins

Pour: 2 C. boiling water over
1 C. raisins

Let sit

Mix: 2 C. bran
2 C. whole wheat flour
1 1/2 T. baking powder
1 T. cinnamon

Mix: 2 T. oil
1 t. vanilla
1/2 C. agave
(or 1/4 C. agave and
1/4 C. molasses)

Mix: wet into the dry ingredients

Add: raisins and hot water

Fold In: 1/2 pint
fresh raspberries or
cranberries or
blueberries or
gooseberries

Fill: Greased muffin cups

Bake: at 350° until the center holds it's shape

Drizzle: agave over the tops as they come out of the oven.

Buckwheat Eggless Pancakes

Most people who have wheat allergies can enjoy buckwheat.
A bonus is that buckwheat is one of the few Alkaline grains

Mix: 1 C. buckwheat flour

1 t. baking powder

2 T. milled, soaked flax seeds

1 1/2 C. water, rice, soy or nut milk

1/4 t. cinnamon (optional)

Grease: cast iron griddle with butter or canola oil

Pour: A couple of Tbs. of the batter on several spots on the grill

Turn: the pancakes over as soon as you can

Serving Suggestions: Buckwheat has a full, hearty flavor which, for some, is enough in and of itself. Others will like agave drizzled over the top.

Granola

Back in the 70s in Amherst, MA was the beginning of my natural food career. I baked local apple whole wheat muffins and cookies and sold them to the U. Mass Student Center. These were snack foods.

To keep costs down I rented, part-time, a pizza kitchen during the day. Two other hippies shared the space on different shifts.

One of the guys was John Brouchek. He started a business called Good Morning New England Granola. The other fellow was named Aristotle. He made Tofu Pies.

Although neither of them taught me their art, I was around them enough to get inspired to come up with my own. John, for instance mixed maple syrup and oil and baked the granola. I preferred not to cook the oil so I roasted the oats first, then added oil and agave.

My favorite way to eat John's granola was to pour boiling water over it, so it was both soft and crunchy. Aristotle was my inspiration for Banana Tofu Pie. Aristotle didn't stay in business long. He went off to become a Naturopath.

I've lost track of both of these creative souls, but I moved the handmade wooden chairs that Aristotle's dad built, from Amherst, MA to my kitchen here, 30 years later, in Pagosa.

Granola

Mix: in a large bowl
8 C. thick rolled oats
1 C. pecans, walnuts or almond pieces

Spread: into an ungreased stainless or pyrex baking pan

Bake: at 350° until the oats start turning brown

Remove: from the oven

Add: 1 C. agave or
1 C. maple syrup or
1 C. barley malt
1/2 C. oil
1 T. vanilla
1 C. unsweetened shredded coconut
1 C. sunflower or pumpkin seeds

Mix: liquid into the dry ingredients. While the granola is still warm, move it around so that it won't stick the bottom of your pan

Cool

Add: 1 C. raisins or currants
1/2 C. unsulfured apricots or dried apples

Store: in a glass jar

Variations: For pie or fruit crisp: If you are going to use some of the granola for making pie crusts or fruit crisp, only use the first group of ingredients, as the raisins tend to burn when baked

For trail mix add:
1/2 C. unsweetened carob chips
1/2 C. unsweetened dried pineapple chunks
1/2 C. unsweetened papaya pieces
1/2 C. date pieces.

Hot Cereal

When you boil up your morning hot cereal (oatmeal, quinoa, amaranth, millet, wheat berries) think of adding cinnamon, ginger, cardamom and some soaked nuts (almonds, filberts, pecans).

The spices will help you digest the grains. The nuts will complete the protein and will slow down the glycemic effect of the grain.

Muffins

Mix: 4 C. whole wheat flour
1 1/2 T. baking powder
1/2 C. oil or butter
1/2 C. agave
2 C. liquid (apple cider, water, grain or nut milk)

Variations: If you use dry fruit (raisins, dried apricots, pineapple, papaya, figs, prunes) use the above recipe

If you use juicy fruit (nectarines, fresh peaches, fresh pineapple) use less liquid

If you use heavy fruit (mashed bananas) use more baking powder

If you use berries (raspberries, blueberries) roll them in flour before adding them at the end so they will stay suspended evenly in your muffins

I like to use a canola spray inside paper muffin cups. This way the muffins come out of the pan easily and the paper muffin cups don't stick to the muffins

Adding vanilla, lemon rind, cinnamon, cardamom will complement your fruit. Using just grains and nuts, omitting fruit is better food combining.

Whole Wheat Pancakes
This is a basic pancake recipe

Mix:
- 1 C. whole wheat flour
- 1 t. butter or oil
- 1/2 T. soaked, blended flax seeds
- 1 t. baking powder
- 1/2 t. cinnamon
- 1 1/4 C. soy, rice or hazelnut milk
- 1/2 t. vanilla

Grease: cast iron griddle with butter or canola oil

Pour: a couple of tablespoons of the batter on several spots on the grill

Fry: batter by spoonful on lightly oiled griddle or in a frypan

Turn: the pancakes over as soon as they begin to brown

Sweeten: the top, when cooked, with agave and pecan pieces

Variations: You can flour 1/2 cup fresh raspberries, blueberries, apples or fresh apricot pieces before cooking small amounts of batter on a greased, cast iron griddle flipping the pancakes over to cook both sides.

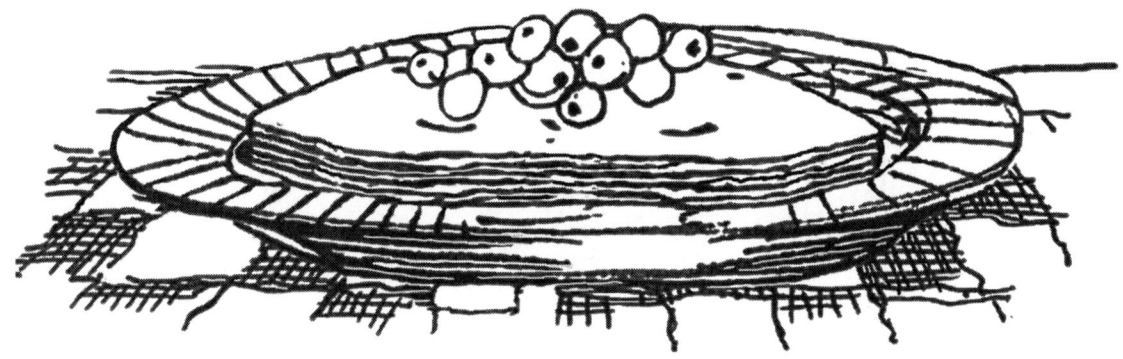

Beverages

Freshly made juices are most beneficial when drunk right away. Do not make a batch to refrigerate for a week!

Again, fresh juice is one of the BEST ways to start your day. You can use the pulp in your compost.

Please do not juice veggies and fruit. You will no longer have an alkaline beverage and most likely will be gassy.

Green Drink

This is the BEST way to begin your day

Juice: 1 European cucumber or 2 regular cukes
1 bunch parsley
1 carrot
4 to 6 stalks celery (high in minerals)

Variations: Add to green drink
cilantro
kale
ginger
garlic
comfrey leaves and stalk
cabbage
beets
beet greens

Note: Juicing cabbage by itself and drinking it right away can help tremendously with ulcers. The juice tends to stink. The first taste requires some getting-used-to, but from then on, expect a miracle!

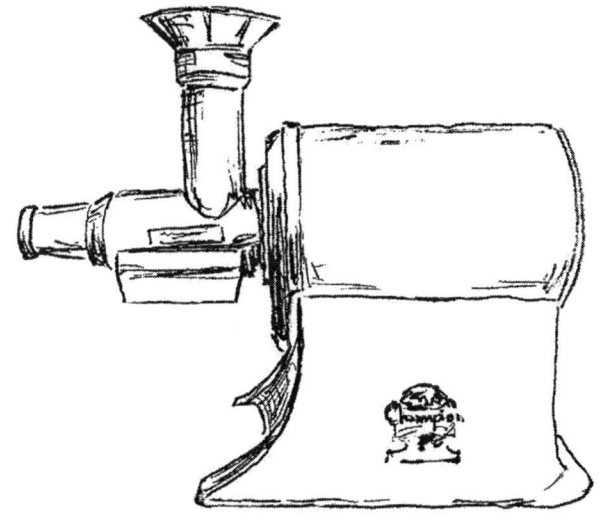

Nut Milks

Most of the nut, grain and soy milks on the market are sweetened (which makes them acid), but, it's easy to make your own!

Cover: 1 C. almonds with clean water. Let them soak overnight

Water: your plants with the water you throw off

Place: the nuts in the blender

Cover: the nuts with water and whiz

Add: more water so that the nuts produce a 'milk'

Strain: the mixture. You now have a nut milk

Variations: Add cinnamon or cardamom for variety

For a delicious warm "milk", heat some nut, soy or rice milk and add carob powder to taste

For protein drinks, follow the same procedures as above but don't strain the nuts out. You can also add Nuttiva Hemp Protein Powder to your drink.

Protein Drink

An Omega-3 Drink
This will be thick and filling

Soak: 1/3 C. flax seeds overnight in 3 C. water

Add: enough water to allow the thick gel to blend easily

1 T. hulled hemp seeds or hemp protein powder

1 t. fresh ginger root or 1/2 t. ground cinnamon if you like the flavor

Blend: into a frothy drink

Variation: Add 1/3 C. soaked almonds or filberts for taste and additional protein.

Banana Smoothie

Children as well as adults delight in this non-dairy thick drink

Pour: into your blender
2 C. fresh apple cider

Add: 1 or 2 ripe bananas
1/2 t. vanilla

Blend: 30 seconds and voila!

Pour: into a glass and sprinkle with cinnamon

Variations: Add a few raspberries, strawberries, pineapple chunks or blueberries for a delectable treat.

Festive Fruit Punch

Mix: together in a punch bowl
4 quarts apple raspberry juice
1 gallon fresh apple cider
1 quart seltzer water

Slice: 2 kiwi fruit
2 lemons

Float: the sliced fruit on top of the punch, as needed

Add: a few strawberries and ice cubes and serve!

Teas

*There are so many herbs with healthy qualities just waiting to be brewed.
The only use I have for black tea because it's fermented is to use it as the
liquid needed for henna powder for my hair*

Pour: boiling water over herbs
Simmer: roots and barks for 20 minutes
Steep: tea for 15 minutes before drinking

- **Chamomile:** to help calm the nerves, especially before sleep
- **Hibiscus:** for the tea's color and for skin and complexion
- **Hollyhocks:** has diurectic properties
- **Jasmine flowers:** for the taste and to reduce tissue masses
- **Lavender flowers:** for the charm, delicate flavor and for calming nerves
- **Lemon verbena:** soothes nerves, especially before sleep
- **Licorice:** use the Chinese version (glycyrrhizu uralensis) to detox the body and to help come off prednisone
- **Mullein flowers:** for cleaning out the lymphatics
- **Olive leaf:** is bitter and is antiseptic
- **Parsley:** to clean the blood
- **Peppermint:** for upliftment and upset stomach
- **Red clover flowers:** for estrogen
- **Saffron:** can help with depression, coughs, asthma, and devotion
- **Sage:** to become very wise! (for calm and clear thinking)
- **Turmeric powder:** for the lungs and antibiotic properties

Variations: See if you like the taste of star anise and organic orange peel
The best alkalizing tea is made with warm water and fresh lemon juice!

*If you use a teacup without a handle
you'll not burn your tongue with tea that's too hot*

Sun Tea

Make sun tea by putting herbs in a glass jar.
Leave it in the summer sun for the day…and you will have delicious tea!

Wheat Grass Juice

Wheat grass juice is one of the BEST foods on the planet! It is alkaline and is high in protein, vitamins, and minerals. It detoxes the body and is a tonic. The only problem I find with it is its taste...too sweet.

There are several ways to obtain the juice. Most health food stores will juice the grass for you. I recommend mixing the 1 oz. shot into 8 oz. of water because of its potency.

Many health food stores sell wheat grass in pots so you can take it home to juice. It is also sold as "cat grass".

Or, you can soak wheat berries, sprout them, and grow the grass on a thin layer of soil, uncovering the sprouts when they are 3 inches tall, exposing them to the sun, indoors.

If you don't want to invest in a wheat grass juicer, which presses the moisture out of the grass, use your blender.

Cut: a handful of wheat grass

Cut: the bunch into 2 inch lengths with scissors

Place: the cut grass in a blender

Cover: the grass with water

Add: 2 fresh sprigs of mint (to lighten the flavor)

Liquefy: the mixture

Strain: the "brew" into a glass

Serving Suggestion: Drink juice immediately.

You will be a powerhouse for the remainder of the day!

Yogurt Beverage
This drink is especially good during the summer

Mix: 2 C. yogurt with
1 C. water or fruit juice
1 t. agave (optional)
1/3 C. mashed fresh fruit (strawberries, raspberries, blueberries)
1/4 t. vanilla

Pour: into a glass and enjoy!

Sprinkle: the top with powdered cardamom.

Mindful Eating

Speaking from my Caucasian American part, I see that too many of us eat not for nutrition and energy, but for distraction and comfort. Food can be our medicine or our poison. What does this mean?

When we eat while driving or watching TV are we trying to assuage our loneliness, fear or stress? We tend to eat more when we distract ourselves in these ways. On the other hand we can choose a quiet place where we can enjoy chewing, the food's taste, texture and benefit for us. How can we be grateful to all the microbes of the earth, devas, forces of nature, farmers and cooks if our attention is on getting to our destination or on a movie?

All the participants who helped grow and prepare the "carrot" have placed attention energy into that "carrot". The "carrot" is the carrier for this energy, which if properly digested, allows us to thrive. This seems basic…to be present, thoughtful and appreciative of all who have given to us, so that we may continue living and giving.

When we eat mindfully we tend to eat less. The fulfillment part of our brain gets satiated. Ideally we would be filling 2/3 of our stomachs. Roughly speaking, this is two hands full of cooked food.

To me, eating to fullness is missing the mark. We want to be full of energy, joy, truth, love, wisdom…not food. Being full of food replaces the space that allows for the real satisfaction in life.

So, do I always eat this way? No.

Is it my ideal? Yes.

Setting the Mood

A candle is lit with intention. Tune into the occasion and guests even if it's you and only you that you are cooking for. What will make this meal bring smiles? Knowing what others like or need helps. Cooking is not for impressing others with our abilities but can be a loving ménage-a-trois amongst the cook, the eaters and nature. Presenting a fun, beautiful, balanced, easy to digest meal which leaves palates and bellies feeling good is a noble intention.

Usually I let an idea for an entrée come to me then work around it. Let's say that guests are arriving from a distance during the snowy winter. Indian red lentil soup won't be spoiled if it needs to wait, and its warmth and spices will be soothing. Of course, to complete the protein, some Indian Basmati rice with cumin seeds will accompany the soup. Steamed kale or collards can go into the soup at the last minute. A mixed baby green salad is a must for enzymes…and what for dessert?

Dessert…usually people are quite satisfied with such a meal topped off with a cup of ginger tea. But then again, some have a yen for a sweet…so perhaps Ginger Dunking Cookies or Sesame-Coconut Candies.

Now the cooking music goes on. For this meal it will come from India, either a sweet meditative sound or lively Bangra dancing music.

Usually I begin by making the dessert. This way it won't pick up any flavorings of onion or garlic from the entrée. Then the entrées are cooked. Then the tea, and finally the salad is put together.

Even if a meal is a potluck, I like having the tableware set up before people arrive. It gives a sense of caring to the meal. Using cloth napkins seems to be out of the ordinary nowadays, but even for outside meals, I like the feel and the ecology of cotton.

I like doing my own dishes. People can help clear the table but putting on some Mozart the next morning prolongs the conversation and good feeling from the previous evening. It helps me savor and appreciate my friends. In the quiet of warm sudsy water I wish them well.

Appetizers

Babaganouche Dip

Slice: 3 eggplants in half, sprinkling them lightly with salt

Turn: eggplants skin side down on a towel for 1/2 hour

Pat off: the liquid that the salt has extracted

Bake: at 350° face down in a glass dish filled with 1/4 inch water until the center is soft (about 30 minutes)

Scrape: cooled eggplant 'meat' out of the skins

Mix: 4 C. of the eggplant 'meat'
1 C. tahini (sesame seed butter)
juice of 2 fresh lemons
3 cloves of garlic, diced
a dash of real salt
a few drops of roasted sesame oil
a pinch of cayenne

Taste: dip to see of you can taste the eggplant, tahini, lemon and then garlic. Add more of whatever might be needed to bring it into balance

Cut: whole wheat pita bread in half with scissors and cut the halves into triangles

Pour: babaganouche into a wooden bowl

Sprinkle: the top with some cayenne or garnish with black olives and parsley

Drizzle: some olive oil over the top of the babaganouche

Place: the pita bread around the bowl and dip in!

Variation: In France they serve this variation: It's called Vegetarian Caviar. It is prepared the same way as Babaganouche but the tahini is omitted. It is served very cold with lots of lemon and crushed garlic. Both varieties are enhanced if the eggplant is sliced and roasted on a grill rather than baked.

Baked Brie and Crackers

Make: a pie crust for a 3 lb. Brie

Cut: 1/3 C. butter into
1 C. whole wheat flour

Add: a few drops of cold water so that the dough holds together

Mix: dough with your hands

Roll out: dough on floured counter top dough should be the size of the Brie including the sides. (About 1/4 inch thick)

Place: Brie on a greased round pan. (A pizza pan is perfect)

Spread: a thin layer of prepared mustard over the Brie

Cover: Brie with the crust you have made, cutting off any extra crust as it touches the pan. Make the crust "hug" the Brie

Brush: crust with a beaten egg white

Place: a few almonds on the crust to decorate the Brie

Make: a few shallow slits in the crust but don't cut the Brie

Bake: at 375° on the top rack until the brie begins to swell and the crust is a golden brown

Serving Suggestions: Serve hot, with sturdy crackers (stoned wheat crackers have worked well), placed around the Brie

Suggest that your guests begin with dipping for the cheese in the center of the brie so that the cheese will stay intact.

Reheat the Brie if needed.

Cheese Fondue

Although cheese fondue is thought to be one of the most romantic and elegant European dishes, it is interesting to learn that the fondue originated in the peasant population of Switzerland, where, at the end of the week, crusts of old cheese were melted down and stale bread was used to dip into the cheese. (Fondue means "melted".)

Today, even non-dairy folks can enjoy this treat. Fondue is especially good with hot ginger tea, on a cold winter's night, when you can share your time and self with close family and friends

- **Use:** a fondue pot, chafing dish or regular pan
- **Cut:** a clove of garlic in half
- **Rub:** the garlic around the inside of the pan
- **Pour:** enough water into the pan to have a 1/4 inch layer
- **Cut:** or grate 1 package of cheddar soyakaas (soy cheese)
- **Melt:** cheese slowly in the pan over medium heat
- **Add:** a pinch of cayenne or nutmeg
  more water if it becomes too thick
- **Keep:** the fondue warm by putting it over a warming candle or over hot water in a chafing dish
- **Dip:** into the fondue any of the following using long forks
  some whole wheat day old French bread
  Ezekial sprouted tortillas.

In our family, this is our traditional Christmas Eve dinner

Chili Bean Dip

Soak: 1 C. dry kidney beans overnight and drain

Simmer: beans until soft

Mash: the beans

Stir Fry: 1 diced onion in olive oil
4 cloves chopped garlic
1 T. chili powder (or to taste)

Mix: fried mixture into mashed beans, stirring the mixture for a minute. If it seems too dense add a little water

Add: salt to taste

Cool

Add: 1 finely chopped tomato
1/2 bunch chopped fresh cilantro

Pour: into the bottom of a glass or ceramic pie dish as a base for the Guacamole-Bean Dip or to eat dipping celery sticks in it.

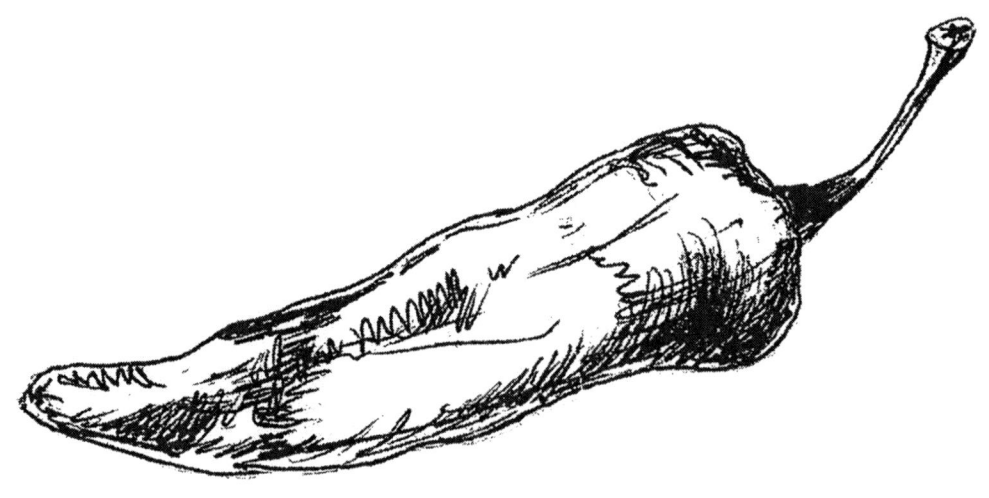

Crackers

Combine: 2 C. whole wheat flour
1/2 C. oil or butter
1 egg (optional)
1 T. thyme
1 T. basil
1 t. salt
1/2 T. baking powder
1/4 C. water
1/2 t. garlic powder

Mix: all the ingredients

Roll out: to 1/8 inch thick on a greased cookie sheet

Cut: desired shapes with a knife, juice glass or cookie cutter and remove dough between shapes

Sprinkle: the top with sesame, poppy seeds and thyme

Press: seeds into the dough

Make: little holes in the tops of the crackers with a fork

Bake: at 350° until brown

Note: Watch them carefully as they cook quickly

Variation: It is possible to make these without eggs by adding a little more water.

Egg Rolls

Egg rolls are easy and fun to make

Buy: some egg roll wrappers

Steam lightly: broccoli
　　　　　　shredded cabbage
　　　　　　carrots
　　　　　　garlic
　　　　　　celery

Cook: some bean thread noodles

Place: about 3 Tbs. of the veggie mixture about 2 inches in from a corner of the wrapper

Lay: a few bean threads over the veggies

Roll: the corner over the veggies and then bring in the two side corners

Moisten: the remaining corner so it will stick to the wrapper and finish rolling it tightly

Pan fry: in coconut oil until brown, turning often

Serving Suggestion: Serve with hot Chinese mustard.

Endives

In your supermarket you can find endive lettuce which is curly and bitter. Hopefully, you can also find endives. Because they are tricky to grow, they can be pricey, but treating them as a delicacy makes them go a long way for all to enjoy

Separate: the "leaves"

Arrange: the leaves in a circle on a large round plate

Filling Suggestions: Drop one teaspoon of any of the following fillings onto the wide opening of the leaf:

> Freshly finely shredded carrots with lemon juice, olive oil, garlic and a small piece of an olive
>
> Babaganouche*
>
> Crumbled steamed tofu with Sesame Dressing*
>
> Pico de gallo*
>
> Cooked Rice mixed with walnuts

Serving Suggestion: The French eat endives by removing one "leaf" at a time, dipping them in a sauce made of olive oil, lemon juice and garlic.

Guacamole

Guacamole is an avocado dip with Mexican flair!

Scoop out: the pulp of 3 ripe small avocados. (The giant variety available nowadays is not as tasty)

Mash: the avocados

Add: juice of 1 lemon
1 minced clove of garlic

Mix: and you have a dip

Correct: for taste

Note: Make sure that the basic taste is right. You want to be able to taste the avocado, some lemon and garlic

Serving suggestion: Serve with fresh veggies such as celery, zucchini or carrots

Note: Leave the pit in the center to prevent the guacamole from turning brown

Variations: Add more lemon juice or garlic according to your taste

A pinch of salt will bring out all of the delicate flavors

Top the guacamole with some sour cream and a pinch of chili powder

Mix in some diced tomatoes and add a pinch of cumin powder

Best of all, scrape the dark green part next to the inside of the skin of the avacado and rub it onto the skin of your face to moisturize and nourish your complexion.

Guacamole-Bean Dip

This is a sure party success!

Grease: the bottom of a glass or ceramic pie pan slightly with olive oil

Mix: 2 C. cold refried beans
chili powder
garlic
onions

Spread: bean mixture into the bottom of the pan

Put: a layer of guacamole on the top

Note: Use the Guacamole* recipe on the previous page

Pour: salsa over the top

Serving suggestion: Serve with celery sticks for dipping

Variation: Use mashed black beans with cumin, garlic and olive oil.

Hummus

Wash: 1 C. garbanzo beans

Soak: beans overnight

Pour: water off

Cook: the beans in 4 C. water

Note: Use a deep pot for cooking, as the water will froth

Simmer: the beans for 2 hours or until soft

Blend: beans in a blender with just enough of the bean water to make a thick mixture

Add: 1 C. tahini
juice of 1 or 2 lemons
4 cloves of crushed garlic
pinch of salt
few drops of roasted sesame oil
pinch of cayenne

Note: What you are looking for is the ability to taste the garbanzos, the lemon and the garlic with enough salt to bring out the fullness of each ingredient. The tastes are subtle, so you can add more lemon or garlic

Serving suggestion: Serve in a wide wooden bowl where you have at least 2 to 3 inches of bowl left above the hummus

Variations: Drizzle olive or sesame oil over the top and fresh lemon juice
Decorate with some fresh parsley
Use triangles of pita bread or celery sticks to dip into the hummus appetizer.

Jello-1 (Aspic)

In my twenties I was so proud to bring my American contribution to the family dinner…tomato aspic. My French family could not, would not taste it, and couldn't have it on the dinner table! To the French it was raw liver.

I am not a huge gelatin fan but for the convalescing it's a better choice than the sugary and artificially flavored sweetened packages

Sprinkle: 2 envelopes of gelatin onto 1/2 C. of cold tomato juice

Boil: another cup of the juice and add it to the cold gelatin after it has set for at least 1 minute

Mix

Add: another cup of juice or vegetable broth

Pour: into individual servings, (glasses or cups) or into a bowl

Place: in the fridge or cold spot until it sets

Variations: For vegetable jello, juice some veggies (parsley, carrots, celery, and cucumber)

For fruit jello, prepare using fresh fruit juice.

Pâté

This of course, is a vegetarian version of the famous goose liver pâté

Boil: in 2 C. water
1 C. French lentils (tiny green/brown)
1/2 an onion
1 clove of garlic

Sauté: 1 large onion, diced
6 cloves of garlic

Strain: the lentils well, after they are soft

Blenderize: lentils, onions and garlic

Add: 2 pinches of real salt
a healthy dose of freshly ground pepper
1/2 bunch of fresh parsley
1 T. olive oil

Pour: into an oiled enamel 6" round baking pan

Bake: for an hour at 350°.

Note: It will thicken as it cools

Serving suggestion: Serve on home-made crackers or on celery.

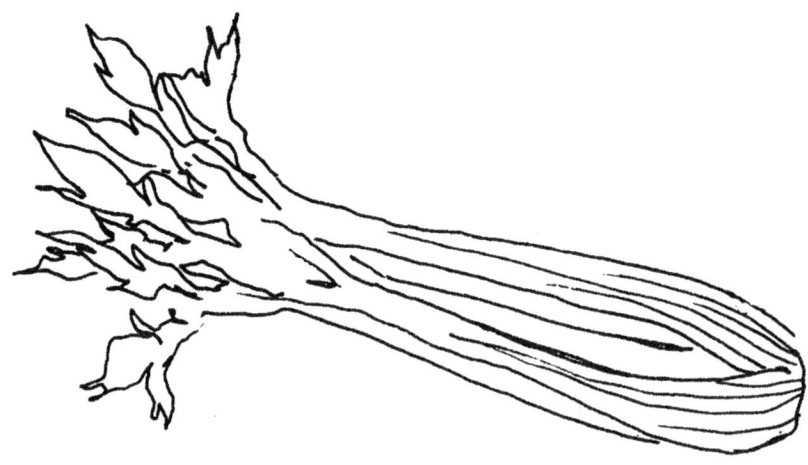

Pis à la Dière

In the South of France where my mother and grandmother were born, they celebrate during the summer months, the feast of the village's patron saint, with a week-end of festivities including an outside ball in the village square.

They parade a large statue of their patron saint through the streets. A toast is given by the mayor of the village followed by an 'apéritif'. Typically Pastis, an anise beverage, is served with olives from Nice or its surrounding villages and if one is very fortunate, Pis à la Dière (French onion Pie) is offered.

Pis à la Dière can be found in most bakeries in the South of France. Typically it's made with onions, olives from Nice and anchovies. Sometimes the crust is like pizza dough and sometimes its one of those indescribably good but impossible to make layered crusts. Here's my version, which seems to be a hit, hot or cold, here in the U.S.

Layer: on a sheet cake pan
sheets of filo dough brushing between each sheet with olive oil

Pan fry: 6 large onions in olive oil
a sliced bulb of garlic

Remove: onions from skillet

Note: Onions should be translucent and some of the onions a little brown. (My French grandmother, Graine, told me about this perfect cook-point)

Leave: the juice created during the cooking process behind in the pan

Spread: onions over the filo dough

Cover: the top with
thyme,
real salt
freshly ground pepper

Place: 1/2 of a 'Niçoise' olive (or oil-cured olive) for each portion on the onion (So perhaps you'll have 12 to 16 portions for your sheet cake pan)

Bake: at 350° until the filo is cooked through and lightly browned as are some of the onions

Drizzle: top with olive oil

Cut: pieces with scissors

Serving suggestion: Serve hot, warm, cold, or re-heated.

Alternate Pis à la Dière Crust

Prepare: a quick bread batter

Mix: together with enough water for the batter to stick together
4 C. whole wheat flour
1 C. olive oil
1 T. baking powder
1/2 t. salt
2 T. basil
1 T. thyme

Spread: quick bread batter on oiled parchment paper

Prepare: onion mixture as described in Pis à la Dière

Cover: bread batter with the cooked onions

Top: as described in the previous recipe

Bake: as you would the filo dough for Pis à la Dière

Note: See baking instructions (above).

Roasted Pepitas
(pumpkin seeds)
Eddie, our car mechanic as well as the local librarians have given these rave revues, holiday season after holiday season

Warm: a cast iron pan

Cover: the bottom with pepitas (use about 1/2 pound)

Stir continuously

Remove: the pan from the stove when pepitas begin to pop

Sprinkle: with small amounts of Bragg Liquid Aminos
 chili powder
 cumin powder
 garlic powder

Add: more (or less) dry seasonings according to your taste

Stir: with a wooden spoon so that each seed is covered. Each time you add an ingredient, sprinkle just enough to cover the pepitas

Note: Work quickly while the Pepitas are still hot

Store: in a glass jar when cool

Serving suggestion: Serve as an appetizer or snack food during cold weather

Variation: You can also roast almonds, pecans or sunflower seeds but roast them separately.

Salmon in Steamed Rice Wrappers

Poach: 1/2 lb. wild caught Pacific salmon

Shred: salmon with a fork like you would tuna

Add: 1 finely chopped garlic clove
1 T. chopped chives
1 t. grated ginger
1 T. finely chopped parsley or cilantro
2 t. sesame oil
1 t. Bragg Liquid Aminos
2 t. sesame oil
1/4 of the juice of a lemon

Boil: water in the pan you are going to set your bamboo steamer on

Dip: into this water, as it begins to boil a round rice wrapper

Note: Use the same rice wrappers you'd use to make spring rolls

Remove: the wrappers from the water as soon as they begin to soften

Place: a wrapper on a wooden board

Fill: the wrapper with 2 Tbs. of the salmon mixture

Note: Wrap the packet like you would an eggroll by folding in the 2 ends then rolling it

Place: the wrap in your bamboo steamer seam side down

Repeat: until you have used all the salmon

Steam: the complete salmon wraps for 10 minutes

Serving suggestion: Serve as an appetizer with a Bragg Liquid Aminos Garlic Ginger Sauce.

Stuffed Grape Leaves

Steam: fresh grape leaves

Note: You may also used leaves you have canned. If you can your own leaves, use fresh lemon juice in the glass jars along with the water

Cook: 1/2 C. rice in 1 C. water

Note: You will have 1 cup cooked rice

Mix: 1 C. cooked rice
juice of 1 lemon
1 T. fresh chopped parsley
salt and pepper to taste or 1 T. chopped cured olives
2 T. pine nuts
1 T. finely chopped garlic

Place: 1 T. of the mixture in the center of each leaf

Roll: sides inward, then roll the rest of the grape leaf over the rice from front to back, so that you have an 'egg roll' wrap

Drizzle: olive oil and lemon juice over top

Serving suggestion: Serve at room temperature or cool

Variations: Add 1 T. ginger grated
   Use some Bragg Liquid Aminos and chopped cilantro instead of parsley and salt.

Tartar

One of my younger brothers, James, lives in northern California. He loves taking classes and is a fabulous home-cook. After his first class, I called him and he said, "We made beef tartar." "Oh, yeah?" was my response. "Why would you go to a cooking class to eat raw meat?" He laughed. "No, beet tartar. It's beets with herbs." Here's my version

Boil: a beet or beets until tender

Peel: the beets

Cut: into 2 inch pieces

Chop: beet pieces in a food processor until the pieces are the size of "chopped meat"

Add: to taste finely chopped

parsley

garlic

green (spring) onion or the green stem of a sprouting onion

Add: a little thyme

a little olive oil

lemon juice

Serving Suggestions: You can eat this as-is, on a salad or on large, thinly sliced carrot rounds

You can also form it into a heart, making it a "heart beet"

Cook some tofu in the beet juice to turn the tofu pink.

Even if you don't care for beets, this is worth a try!

Yogurt Cheese

This is the easiest cheese you can make, and it is most delicate and versatile

Purchase: 1 quart of high quality plain yogurt (the kind that only contains milk and culture as ingredients)

Line: a large bowl with a double layer of cheesecloth

Pour: yogurt into the cheesecloth

Gather: the top edges of the cheesecloth together

Tie: the top edges of the cheesecloth to make a bundle

Hang: the cheesecloth bundle overnight over your sink, or over a pan, to catch the whey (you can use the whey as a liquid for other cooking). In the morning, remove the cheese from the cheesecloth

Refrigerate

Serving Suggestions: Use this cheese as a spread on crackers or as a filling in celery stalks

Variations: Add some herbs (thyme, basil, parsley) some chopped garlic and a pinch of salt and cayenne before refrigerating.

Grate in 1 T. ginger

Use some Bragg Liquid Aminos and chopped cilantro instead of parsley and salt.

Soups

The healthiest way to eat soups is to barely boil the veggies. A tastier soup requires browning the veggies in olive oil, then adding them to the water. If you just boil the veggies, add olive oil and lemon juice just before serving, as well as parsley or cilantro garnishes.

In France, a traditional soup, eaten for the supper meal, is made by blending a vegetable soup (with or without potatoes) with an electric wand. This creates small pieces of vegetables (often leftovers) instead of liquefying them in a blender. Then you can add herbs, thyme, and/or basil, again adding olive oil at serving time.

If children don't want to eat vegetables, soup often is acceptable.

Basic Veggie Soup

Fill: a large pot with 10 C. water

Add: 1 large onion, chopped
1 C. celery, chopped
2 carrots, cubed
4 cloves garlic
1/2 bunch chopped parsley

Simmer: 25 to 45 minutes or until the veggies are tender

Add: Salt and pepper to taste

Variations: Add a mixture of any of the following
2 potatoes, diced
1/2 C. rice
1 parsnip, diced
1 rutabaga, diced
1/2 celery root, diced
1/2 C. barley with 2 bay leaves
1/2 C. yiyi ren (Chinese barley)
1/2 lb. cubed tofu
1 leek, sliced
1 zucchini, sliced

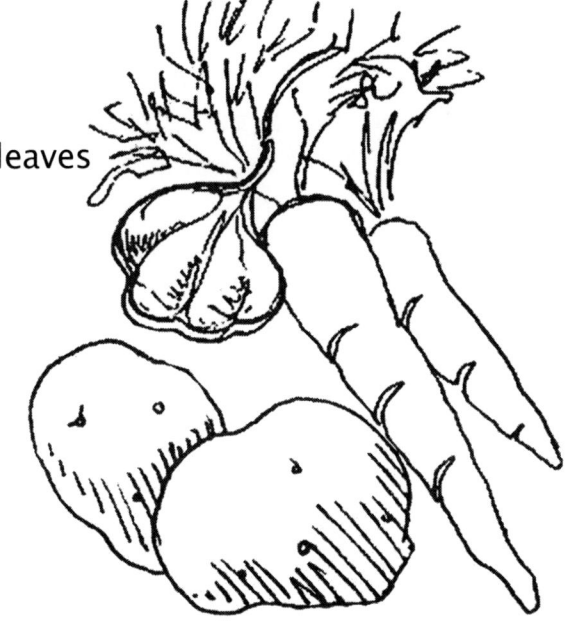

Black Bean Soup

Sha:nta adds a couple pinches of chipotle powder for a spicier soup

Soak: 1 cup black beans overnight

Drain

Water: your plants with the water you strain off

Simmer: the beans in 8 C. water with
- 1 onion, diced
- 6 cloves garlic
- 2 carrots, cubed
- 2 T. cumin
- 4 slices fresh ginger
- 1 parsnip, diced

Cook: until the beans are soft

Note: This will take a few hours on your stove or overnight in a crock pot

Serving Suggestions: Serve with a round slice of lemon and a little olive oil for each bowl.

The Best Carrot Soup
This makes a thick, delicious, creamy soup

Pan fry: in some olive oil for 5 minutes:
- 1 large onion, chopped
- 1 1/2 lbs. carrots, cubed
- 1/2 t. turmeric
- 1/2 t. cardamom powder
- 4 cloves garlic
- 4 slices fresh ginger

Cover: with water

Add: 1/2 C. red lentils

Simmer: until the lentils are soft

Blend: the soup in a blender

Serving Suggestion: Just before serving, add a little olive oil, fresh lemon juice, salt to taste and fresh cilantro

Variations: Use thyme or rosemary.

Carrot-Cabbage Soup
This makes a wonderful winter soup

Shred: 1/2 red cabbage

Add:
- 4 carrots, sliced
- 1 onion, sliced
- 2 cloves of garlic
- 2 slices of fresh ginger

Cover: the veggies halfway with water

Simmer: until the carrots are tender

Put: the vegetables in the blender

Add: enough of the veggie broth to make a thick consistency

Serving Suggestions: When you serve the soup add a little olive oil and some fresh lemon juice (the soup's color will change) Garnish with fresh parsley.

Down-Under Soup

Vegetables grown underground are…yes…grounding, especially if they point downwards. The under-grounders with a double asterisk (**) are really tubers, not exactly vegetables

Here is a list of root vegetables to choose from to make your soup following the recipe on the previous page:

    beets
    burdock root
    carrots
    daikon
    garlic
    ginger root
    horseradish root
    Jerusalem artichoke**
    leeks
    onions
    parsley root
    parsnips
    rutabagas
    sweet potatoes**
    yams**

Add: olive oil before serving

Variations: Blend the soup with a wand or electric blender

    You may want to test 'new-for-you' vegetables (for instance rutabagas) to make sure you like them before you use them as an ingredient in your soup

    Daikon, ginger and horseradish root are "hot" so you need only a sparse amount.

French Onion Soup

Traditionally this soup is made with a beef stock, but it is still delicious with a vegetable or water stock

Brown: in butter, ghee, or olive oil, 2 large yellow onions, sliced

Add: 8 C. vegetable stock or water
1/4 t. freshly ground pepper

Simmer: for 1/2 hour

Serving Suggestions:

Tradition calls for pouring the soup into a casserole dish, covering the top with toasted, sliced French bread which has been covered with Parmesan cheese. The soup is baked until the cheese melts. Each serving includes one of these toasts

If you dare! to step beyond tradition, toast some home-made biscuits, using almond or rice cheese on top

Better yet, enjoy the onion soup as is. If you serve it with quiche and a tossed green salad you will be having an *ou-la-la* meal!

Gazpacho

This is a great summer cold soup

Barely mix in a blender:
- 8 fresh tomatoes
- 2 cucumbers
- 1 green pepper
- 1 bunch fresh parsley

Add: some chopped green onion
salt and pepper to taste

Chill

Serving Suggestions: Serve cold
Top with freshly chopped cilantro.

Lentil Soup

My mother, the night before exams, always fed us lentils to help with our brain function

Bring: to boil 6 C. water

Add:
- 1 onion, chopped
- 2 carrots, chopped
- 1 parsnip, diced – this gives the soup a special flavor
- 2 stalks chopped celery
- 4 cloves of garlic
- 1 C. brown/green lentils
- 2 T. cumin powder
- salt and cayenne to taste

Simmer: until the lentils break down

Variations: Some folks like adding diced potatoes
If you have sensitive intestines omit the cumin.

Matzo Ball Soup

During their exodus from Egypt, the Jews realized that the flour and water "dough" which they had hurriedly thrown in their packs, had baked in the desert's heat, making the first matzo or unleavened bread. Matzo is traditionally served at Passover

Make: 10 C. of vegetable broth (from recipe on the following page), keeping the vegetables in the soup

Crumble: into a blender 4 matzo crackers

Whiz: until you have a "meal"

Note: Meal is coarser than flour

Put: the matzo meal into a bowl (about 1 cup of meal)

Pour: 1 C. of vegetable broth over the meal and mix

Add: 1 T. dried parsley flakes
2 T. dried basil
1 T. dried thyme
1 T. garlic powder
1/4 t. real salt
crushed pepper
2 T. olive oil
2 beaten eggs

Note: If you want lighter matzo balls, beat the egg whites separately

Refrigerate: or cool out in the snow, covered, for an hour

Shape: into 1 inch compact balls with wet hands

Drop: matzo balls into the simmering veggie soup

Cook: at a low boil for 30-45 minutes

Freeze: left-over matzo balls for future use.

Vegetable Broth

Simmer: in 10 C. water for 25 minutes
        2 carrots, cubed
        1 onion, chopped
        1/2 bunch of chopped parsley
        2 stalks of celery, sliced
        3 cloves of garlic
        2 T. dried basil

Add: salt and pepper if desired

Serving suggestion: Serve as is or use in cooking.

Split Pea Soup

This is a thick delicious fall or winter soup

Rinse: 2 C. split peas

Place: split peas into a soup pot with 8 C. water

Add:
    1 onion diced and sautéed
    2 cloves of garlic
    4 cubed carrots
    1 leek, sliced
    salt and pepper to taste

Bring: to a boil

Simmer: until the peas break down

Serving Suggestions: Crush some coriander to sprinkle over each serving
    Chipotle is also a fine sprinkle!

Red Lentil Dahl Soup

Boil: in 10 C. water
2 C. red lentils
1 C. unsulphered coconut sreds
2 C. celery, chopped
2 to 3 carrots, chopped
1 onion, diced
6 cloves of garlic
4 inches of cinnamon sticks (add the whole sticks)
2 inches of fresh ginger, sliced
1 t. turmeric
1/2 t. anise powder
1 t. coriander powder
1/2 t. cardamom powder
3 T. dried parsley

Simmer: 1 hour

Add: before serving
fresh cilantro
freshly ground pepper
a dash of olive oil
a little fresh lemon juice

Serving suggestion: Serve with basmati rice for a complete protein

Variations: To personalize the soup to your palate, add any of the following:
- string beans
- zucchini
- leeks
- kale
- broccoli
- burdock root
- celery root or
- fennel.

Potato Leek Soup

Dice: 4 potatoes

Slice: 1 leek after washing it well

Place: veggies in a pot

Cover: with water

Simmer: until potatoes are soft

Put: veggies in the blender

Add: enough potato broth to blend it up to a thick, creamy consistency

Add: salt and pepper to taste

Drizzle: olive oil on it at serving time

Top: with chopped chives or a pinch of nutmeg

Serving suggestion: Serve warm or cold.

Spinach Velouté

Boil: until tender
1 large chopped onion
2 cloves of garlic
4 C. water

Add: 1 lb. of spinach (a bunch or a frozen package)

Boil: until the spinach wilts

Place: veggies in a blender reserving cooking broth

Whiz: mixture

Add: just enough of the broth to make thick consistency

Serving suggestion: Serve with a drizzle of olive oil and a pinch of cayenne.

Soup au Pistou

Pan fry: in olive oil in an enamel pot
    1 diced onion
    2 carrots, diced
    1 potato, diced
    1 turnip, diced
    2 zucchini, sliced
    1 leek, washed and sliced
    2 garlic cloves
    1 C. yellow wax beans
    1 C. green beans

Brown: lightly

Cover: 3/4 of the vegetables with water

Simmer: until the veggies are tender

Add: 1 C. bowtie pasta.

Making the Pistou

Mash: (or finely chop) 6 cloves of garlic

Add: 6 T. finely chopped fresh basil
    3 finely chopped fresh, ripe tomatoes
    1 1/2 C. shredded gruyère or rice "cheese"
    3/4 C. olive oil
    salt and pepper if needed

Serving Suggestion: When the pasta is cooked, serve the soup with a Tbs. of the Pistou in the center of each bowl. Each person can then mix it into their soup.

Minestrone Soup

Make: a soup (following the instructions for basic vegetable soup*) using:

onion, chopped

garlic

carrots, cubed

parsley, chopped

celery, sliced

zucchini, sliced

chick peas that have been soaked in water over night and cooked until tender

Flavor: with dried basil

thyme

oregano

Serving Suggestions: 15 minutes before serving add some cooked pasta of your choice (bowties, macaroni or tortellini)

a little olive oil

salt

pepper

How much herbs?

Use enough so that you can taste them all separately with no overpowering flavor.

Vegetable Soup - 2

Stir fry over low heat in 2 T. sesame or coconut oil
- 1 large onion, cliced
- 4 cloves of garlic
- 2 carrots, diced
- 1 celery stalk, chopped
- 2 parsnips, chopped
- 1 sweet potato, chopped
- 1 burdock root, diced
- 2 beets, diced
- 1/4 shredded cabbage
- 4 slices of ginger
- 1/2 lb. cubed tofu

Add: veggies to 8 C. boiling water and simmer until the vegetables are tender

Add: 1 to 2 T. of Bragg Liquid Aminos

Serving Suggestion: Serve with brown rice.

Salads

Classic Cold Bean Salad

Soak: 2 C. beans overnight

Choose: uncooked beans that are about the same size (black beans, small lima beans, pinto beans) or (mung beans, adzuki beans, small chick peas)

Note: You can water your plants with the bean water in the morning

Cover: beans with fresh water

Simmer: beans until soft

Drain: beans

Place: beans in a bowl

Cool

Add: 1/2 diced red onion
1/2 diced green, yellow or red pepper
2 cloves chopped garlic
1/2 C. chopped celery
juice of 1/2 lemon
4 T. olive oil
salt and pepper to taste

Variation: If you are using mung beans, add 1 t. grated fresh ginger a dash of Bragg Liquid Aminos hot sesame oil.

Dried Lima Bean Salad

This may sound boring, but wait 'til you taste it!

Soak: 2 C. large dried lima beans overnight in 8 C. water

Throw: water onto your plants in the morning

Cover: lima beans with fresh water

Simmer: with 2 bay leaves until the beans are soft

Add: 2 sliced carrots as the beans are getting soft

Note: Cut the carrots on the diagonal so that the slices are elongated

Cool: in cooking liquid

Remove: carrots and lima beans from cooking pot

Drain

Place: In a bowl

Toss: lightly with olive oil

Sprinkle: with thyme

Add: 2 cloves diced garlic
1/2 bunch chopped parsley
salt to taste
a pinch of cayenne

Serving Suggestions: This salad should be moist so feel free to add some of the veggie broth or more olive oil

After the salad has been served once, put the leftovers in the blender. Serve as a dip with fresh lemon juice and drizzled olive oil.

Fresh Carrot-Cabbage Salad

Grate: with a grater, slicer, mandolin or food processor
1/2 medium red cabbage
1 lb. carrots
1 clove garlic

Chop: 1/2 bunch parsley

Mix: ingredients with
the juice of 1/2 a fresh lemon
4 to 6 T. of olive oil

Variations: Add any of the following
1 T. grated ginger
1/2 T. Bragg Liquid Aminos
cilantro

Cool: before serving

Variation: Use the leftovers for a stir-fry with tofu or as egg roll filling.

Carrot-Beet Salad

This is a colorful, refreshing, vitalizing salad

Grate: carrots and cooked beets

Note: 50/50 is a good proportion

Mix in: some olive oil,
fresh lemon juice
minced garlic
chopped parsley
chopped green onion
a touch of Bragg Liquid Aminos (optional)

Serving Suggestions: Place a small portion on top of a green tossed salad

Serve in 1/2 an avocado or on a bed of frisée lettuce.

Cole Slaw

Eliminating the mayo allows for a safer summer picnic slaw

Grate: 1/2 green cabbage
1/4 red cabbage
2 carrots

Add: 1/2 bunch chopped parsley
1 T. finely chopped red onion
1 T. poppy seeds
3 T. olive oil
fresh lemon juice
salt and pepper to taste
1 T. poppy seeds
Bragg Liquid Aminos (optional).

Stuffed Cucumbers

Slice: lengthwise a European cucumber or one that is locally grown, which hasn't been waxed or oiled

Scoop: out the seeds (you can throw the seeds in your compost)

Sprinkle: with dill

Fill: with thinly sliced avocado
finely shredded carrots
sprouts

Sprinkle: with lemon juice
olive oil
Bragg Liquid Aminos

Serving Suggestion: Serve on a bed of quinoa.

Variations: Fill cucumber halves with a curried rice salad topped with unsweetened coconut

Fill cucumber halves with soaked pecans.

Dandelion Salad

A real field green! The way this will make you feel...can be addictive. I think this is why my grandmother lived to be 101! In Valberg, France, when I was 5 years old, Graine taught me how to pick dandelions with my first "Opinel," (a French pocket knife, with a birch wood handle). Every spring, I keep up the tradition, enticing others to join me

Go: to an unpesticided field or lawn with your knife

Dig up: some dandelions

Note: The root of the dandelion is deep, so go down as far as you like because the root is nutritious as well as the green leaves. The younger the plant, the better tasting it is. The older the plant, the more bitter and tough it gets

Wash: the greens well

Scrape: the roots clean

Chop: roots and greens

Mix: with olive oil
a little fresh lemon juice
a hefty amount of chopped garlic

Variation: I add chopped fresh parsley to cut the bitterness

Serving Suggestion: You only need a little bit...maybe 1/2 to 1 cup to rev you up!

Fruit Salad

Cut: 2 fresh mangos into chunks

Add: 1/2 C. sliced coconut (fresh or dried)
1/2 t. freshly grated ginger
1/2 C. date pieces (Logan or Chinese dates from your Asian market) or raisins
1/2 C. nuts (macadamias, almonds, pecans or filberts)

Sprinkle: with the juice of 1/2 lemon

Serving suggestion: Serve in a wine glass with a sprig of fresh mint

Variation: Of course, a few raspberries in this mix would not offend anyone!

Melon Salad

To digest melons, it is best to eat them alone

Create: a melon salad by either cutting the skinned fruit into cubes or scooping balls out with a melon spoon

Use: a variety of colors (cantaloupe, canary, crenshaw, honeydew, musk melon), adding fresh mint, grated ginger and fresh lemon or lime juice

Arrange: melon salad in stemmed glassware

Variation: Place melon back into the melon rinds for a festive mid-afternoon snack full of vitamins A and C.

Mung Bean Sprout Salad

Make: the dressing first

Combine: 2 T. sesame oil
a dash of hot sesame oil
a dash of Bragg Liquid Aminos
1 crushed garlic clove
1/2 t. finely grated fresh ginger
1 T. water
the juice from 1/4 of a fresh lemon

Mix: ingredients

Pour: over 2 to 3 C. fresh mung bean sprouts

Add: a chopped green onion as a garnish

Serving suggestion: Serve with Asian Soup, rice and stir-fried veggies.

Potato Salad

Boil: a mixture of red, purple and white potatoes

Note: Do not peel the potatoes

Cool: until cold enough to handle

Cut: into 1 inch pieces

Coat: each piece lightly in olive oil

Add: salt and freshly ground pepper
finely chopped red onion
fresh parsley, chopped
green onion tops
a dash of fresh lemon juice

Serve: cool or at room temperature

Serving Suggestions: If you have leftovers, you can pan fry the salad in a little olive oil in the morning for hash browns

Note: You can feel comfortable serving this at a summer picnic without worrying that the mayonnaise could go bad.

Curried Rice Salad
This is a very soothing salad

Wash: 2 C. Himalayan Basmati rice three times

Simmer: in 5 C. water

Add: 4 slices fresh ginger
1/2 t. turmeric
1 cinnamon stick
1/2 t. cumin seeds
1/8 t. cardamom powder
3 cloves of garlic
1/2 red onion, cut into small pieces

Cook: covered, until water is absorbed and the surface of the rice has "holes" in it

Remove: from heat

Cover: the rice and let it sit for 20 minutes or until soft

Mix: in just enough olive or light sesame oil to coat each grain of rice

Mix: in 1 C. of dried sliced coconut or shredded coconut if you don't have fresh or large slices

Add: 1 C. frozen or fresh green peas
juice of 1/2 lemon
more oil if needed for a moist salad
salt and pepper to taste

Serving Suggestions: Garnish with chopped green onions.

Sprouted Salad

Sprouting is easy!

You will be augmenting the nutritional value of seeds, beans, greens and nuts, making them more digestible while allowing their protein to be more available when you sprout. They contain vitamins, minerals and amino acids.

Some of the seeds you can sprout are: adzuki, garbanzo beans, lentils, mung beans, peas, pumpkin and sunflower seeds as well as grains (wheat, buckwheat, barley). Eat these when the sprout is as long as the seed.

Alfalfa, broccoli, mung bean, pea, soy bean, radish, red clover and sunflower seeds can be sprouted to 2 to 4 inches

Cover: each kind of seed in a bowl with water

Soak: over night

Rinse: in the morning put the seeds in a glass mason jar with a cheesecloth cover

Place: on a tilted surface so that extra water runs out

Cover: the glass jar with a towel

Rinse: in the evening and morning until the sprouts are the size you want

Expose: to light sprouts which are to be grown 2 to 4 inches when they reach 2 inches in length

Variations: Mix a variety of sprouts (wheat, garbanzo, lentil, sunflower) with olive oil, garlic, lemon juice, parsley, chives

   Mix mung bean, sunflower, broccoli with sesame oil, Bragg Liquid Aminos, cilantro, garlic, ginger, peppers and lemon

   Soak sunflower and pumpkin seeds overnight, blending them up with a dash of Bragg Liquid Aminos, olive oil, garlic, cayenne and lemon, for a live salad dressing or dip.

Tabouleh

Tabouleh is a Middle Eastern cold salad that is easy to make. It is a favorite mid-summer treat, as you can use the garden's fresh veggies. This is an American version, as authentic Tabouleh calls for mostly parsley

Rinse: 4 C. bulgar wheat (cracked wheat)

Cover: with cold water

Soak: for 2 hours

Drain off: extra water

Note: The grains will double and become light and fluffy, yet they will have a crunch

Chop: 1 bunch of parsley
2 large cucumbers
1 bunch green onions
2 large tomatoes
2 C. cooked or sprouted garbanzo beans (optional)

Mix: veggies into the bulgar

Add: 2/3 C. fresh lemon juice
1/2 C. olive oil

Add: just before serving
4 T. freshly chopped mint

Season to taste: You want to enjoy the balance of the wheat flavor, lemon juice, mint and olive oil

Add more lemon juice or oil if needed

A touch of salt and cayenne will ground the salad and help to bring out its subtle tastes

Variations: You can also make this with cooked, cold quinoa, millet or couscous.

Tomato Salad Provençal

This is a classic French way to eat in-season, fresh tomatoes!

Cut: 6 beautiful, ripe tomatoes into chunks

Add: 2 T. chopped fresh onion
1 t. thyme (fresh is best)
1/2 C. freshly chopped basil

Drizzle: with olive oil

Add: salt and pepper to taste
some Niçoise olives

Place: in a clear glass bowl.

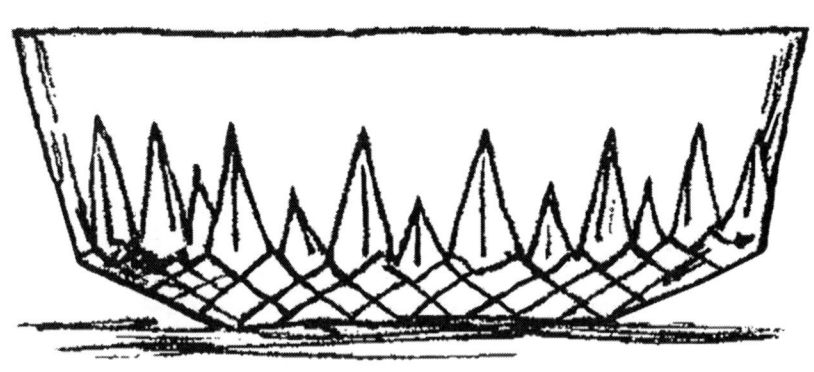

Salad Dressings

Asian Dressing
This is the perfect dressing for a fresh mung bean salad

Mix: 1/2 C. Bragg Liquid Aminos amino acids
1/4 C. water
1 clove of garlic, minced
1/2 T. freshly grated ginger root
a dash of roasted sesame oil.

Avocado Dressing

Mash: 3 ripe avocados

Add: juice of 1 lemon
1 clove of garlic, minced
salt and cayenne to taste

Blend: in blender with enough water to make a thick consistency.

Italian Dressing

Mix: 1 C. olive oil
1/3 C. fresh lemon juice
2 T. water
1 minced clove of garlic
3 sprigs of parsley, chopped
1/2 T. thyme
1/2 T. basil
1/2 T. oregano
pinch of freshly ground black pepper
salt to taste.

Russian Dressing

Mix: 2 C. mayonnaise
1 C. hot salsa
1 T. horseradish
juice of 1/2 lemon.

Sesame Dressing
You can use this on salads, baked potatoes, pasta or veggie burgers or as a dip with pita breads or crudités

Place: 1/2 C. tahini, (crushed sesame butter) in bowl
Mix in: cold water, a little at a time, stirring with a rice paddle
Note: The tahini will thicken, then thin out as you add more water
Add: the juice of 1/2 lemon
1 clove of garlic
a pinch of cayenne and salt
a dash of roasted sesame oil
1/4 lb. boiled, crumbled, drained tofu (optional).

Tofu Mayonnaise
This will be thick and perfect for artichoke dipping

Wiz: 6 oz. (1/2 package) Mori-nu firm, lite tofu (You may have to look for it, as it may not be in the refrigerated section of your market)
1/3 C. olive oil
Note: Use an emersion blender. An electric beater will leave lumps
Add: the juice of 1/2 lemon
a pinch of real salt
a pinch of garlic salt
pepper (if you like)

Wiz again: and voila! You have a soy mayonnaise

Variation: If this mayo is too white for you, add some turmeric.

Variations for Tossed Salad

Using different salad greens enhances nutrition. Most people know that iceberg lacks nutrients, while darker greens, romaine for example, contain minerals, which give us strength, as do beet greens, baby kale and mâche.

I am amazed at the strength of our local deer and elk. They eat mostly greens, as does the gorilla, which is also a powerhouse. Varying your salad greens can be a creative, fun process

Begin: with a large round bowl

Put: some red leaf lettuce around the edges

Fill: the bottom with mixed baby greens

Note: You can make your own mix with some or all of the following:
Romaine
Green leaf
Smaller amounts of radicchio
Frizée
Escarole

Slice: a cucumber and lay it slice by slice on top of the greens

Chop: some celery, laying it over the greens

Chop: some red cabbage and lay it on top of the celery

Slice: an avocado, arranging it over the red cabbage

Grate: some cooked beets and lay them in a ring around the outside edge of the salad

Grate: some carrots, toss with little lemon juice so that they don't turn brown, and make a mound of carrots in the center of the salad

Slice: a green pepper and arrange the rings over the carrots of the salad

Pull: an endive apart and stick the leaves around the outside of the salad wide end down

Leave: the leaves on radishes and place them so that the green tops lay over the outside of the bowl

Sprinkle: the salad with ground flax and sesame seeds that you've milled in an electric coffee grinder

Sprinkle: the top gently with chopped parsley, green onions, and any other herbs of your choice such as fresh basil or thyme

Dress: with a simple olive oil and fresh lemon dressing with garlic

Serving suggestions: Strategically place a few nasturtiums over the top for beauty and a peppery taste

You can also enjoy home grown rose petals, rosemary and sage flowers on your salad

If you are making this for company, your guests will not want to destroy your work of art, so you may have to be the first to partake

Variation: In season, use fresh, new asparagus instead of the endive.

Satiation

Sometimes we might feel hungry after having eaten a good meal. Perhaps this is due to an overgrowth of yeast in our system? The yeast cries out to be fed sweets.

Perhaps this extra hunger comes from a lack in the meal we just ate. Asians have a different way of viewing nutrition. We look at the four food groups; protein, dairy, fruit and vegetables and carbohydrates.

Asians look at two categories; elements and tastes. If our meal contains the five elements, then we are satiated. The five elements are fire, earth, metal, water and wood. Included in this system is to eat different color foods at the same meal.

The six tastes are sweet, sour, salty, bitter, pungent, and astringent. A chart will help you understand this.

	Wood	*Fire*	*Earth*	*Metal*	*Water*
Organ	Liver Eyes	Heart Tongue	Spleen/Pancreas Mouth	Lung Nose	Kidney Ears
Nourishing Taste	**Sour** Lemon Yogurt	**Bitter** Bitter leafy veggies Broccoli Endive	**Sweet** Carbohydrates rice	**Pungent** Horseradish Mustard Peppers	**Salty** Salt
Nourishing Grain	Wheat	Red Millet	Yellow Millet	Rice	Adzuki Beans**
Nourishing Fruit	Plumb	Apricot	Date	Peach	Chestnut
Nourishing Vegetable	Leeks	Scallions	Marshmallow	Onions	Dark Greens

** Adzuki beans are considered a grain in this system

Balance here is the key ingredient. From an alkaline perspective, a satiating dinner could be made with onions and millet topped with scallions along with steamed kale or collards and leeks, with your favorite herbs and a piece of salmon.

In order to feel satiated (a function of the brain), eating while doing nothing else helps. Distractions like eating while driving, watching TV or a movie, or working in front of a computer tend to cause us to eat more to feel satiated.

Sometimes when I sit on the floor to eat a simple meal alone out of a wooden bowl with chopsticks there is an added ingredient...a connection to a population who live and eat simply, taking the time to eat in gratitude. This can be a very nourishing connection.

Eating Locally

In some parts of the U.S. this is easy, as warmth, sun, and water are abundant. Some other parts of the country barely have a growing season. Yet some of these parts may have greenhouses or growing domes. If you have local farmers, please support them. You'll be all the healthier for it.

Do I need to explain that big business had ruined the small farmers of our country and our land and our seeds? City Market has told me that ALL their produce is genetically modified! That means WE are becoming genetically modified.

Buying locally grown produce and herbs means your food hasn't been trucked. This cuts down on planetary pollution which is a way we can choose to be helpful.

Even if you live in a highrise, you can plant a window box with parsley, thyme and chives.

Please eat closer to the garden.

Entrées

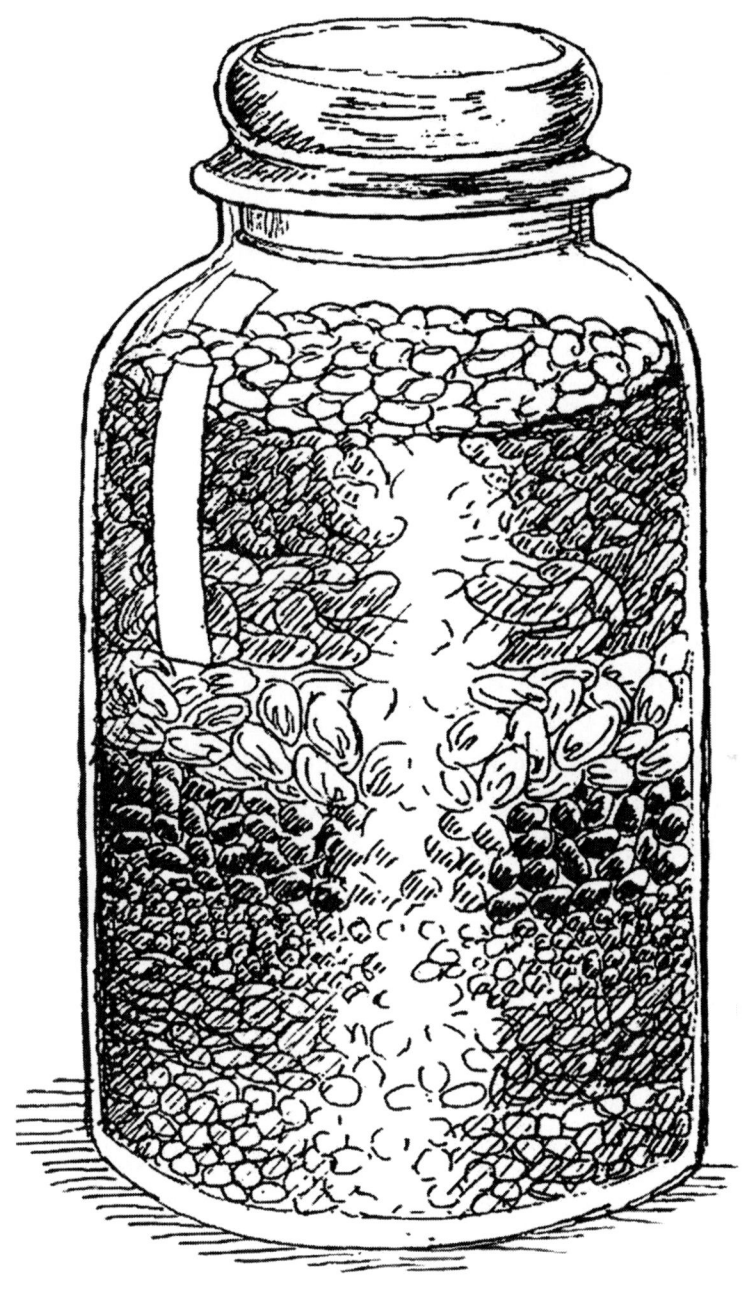

Cooking Beans
Dried beans are easy to cook

Rinse: Always rinse your beans thoroughly in cold water before soaking them

Note: Sometimes there are particles of dirt, or in the case of garbanzo beans, sometimes pebbles mixed in with the beans that you would want to remove!

Soak: beans overnight

Note: Beans usually double in size when they are soaked, so put the desired amount of beans in a bowl, cover them with enough cold water, so that when they swell, the water will still be covering them

Drain off: water in the morning

Place: beans in a pot, pressure cooker, or crockpot

Cover: beans with cold water

Note: If you are making soup, use as much water as you would want liquid broth for your soup. If you just want the cooked beans for refried beans, cover the beans with water so that they are always cooking in the water. (When you are cooking garbanzo beans make sure that you have them in a deep pot because they will foam.) Some people drain off the water after 30 min. to reduce the gassy quality of the beans, then add fresh water to continue the cooking process

Simmer: until the beans are very soft

Note: This may be several hours depending on the type of beans you use

Serving Suggestion: Now that you have the cooked beans, you are ready to use them in your favorite recipe

You can save the bean water to use as a soup base.

Beans

*Here is a list of some easily available beans
with some ideas of how to use them*

Adzuki Beans: small red beans. Use with rice in a ratio of 1:10 (beans to rice). These are good for sprouting and in Asian dishes

Anasazi Beans: medium beans used in soups or stews

Black Turtle Beans: medium beans used with cumin for black bean soup and tacos

Black Eyed Peas: small beans used especially for New Years with collard greens for prosperity

Chick Peas (Garbanzo Beans): these come small or medium size. Use in couscous, tabouleh, humus and minestrone soup

Great Northern Beans: good for refried beans

Kidney Beans: These are rather large and are good for red chili, refried beans and tacos

Lentils: You can find French (tiny), Green/Brown and Red lentils. DO NOT soak lentils. The red are highest in protein and go well with East Indian spices. The other two are good with cumin and in soups

Lima Beans: are white when dry and can be small or large. They work well for a cold salad or as an entrée with garlic and olive oil, or as a dip

Mung Beans: are small green beans. They can be sprouted and used cooked as a soup or in a 1:10 ratio with rice

Navy Beans: are good in soup or in a bean salad

Peas: Do Not Soak. They are green or yellow and split. Whole dried peas can be sprouted. Yellow peas make a delicious Indian curry soup. Green peas are used in soup and are especially tasty cooked over an open fire

Pinto Beans: look specked, red and white and are good in stews, chili, and refried

Soy Beans: Seem to be difficult to digest and are often genetically modified.

Grains

Whole grains provide us with complex carbohydrates. They also contain minerals: iron, magnesium, zinc, copper, manganese, selenium, calcium, the "B" complex vitamins, and amino acids (protein)

Milling or refining them not only reduces their fiber and flavor, but also robs us of important nutrients

Some easily available and delicious grains are: wheat, oats, rye, millet, brown rice, and quinoa. (Wild rice is actually a grass)

These can be ground into flour and used in baking. Some for instance are already commercially used in today's pastas, (wheat, rice, and buckwheat noodles)

There are also some not-so-familiar grains that are easy to prepare:

Whole wheat couscous, for instance is a partially cooked wheat product, to which you add boiling water. After it becomes soft, you can top it with a vegetable sauce

Bulgur is cracked wheat that you can add cold water to and make into tabouleh salad

Kasha is roasted for buckwheat, which is beneficial during the winter, as it helps keep us warm.

Here are some other grains you might enjoy

Amaranath
Barley
Buckwheat
Bulgur (wheat)
Couscous (wheat)
Fonio
Kasha
Millet
Oats
Black, Red or White Quinoa
Rye
Spelt (wheat)
Teff
Wheat Berries
YiYi Ren

Grains can be purchased whole, like wheat berries, which, boiled like rice, make a delicious hot morning cereal or carb for your veggies

Grains also come in flakes. Rye flakes, for instance, will cook up quicker than the whole grain

Grains also come in flour form for baking. So, for those who are gluten intolerant, amaranth flour can be used for making cookies

Some beans can also be purchased in flakes (black beans, pinto beans). Some beans are available in flour form (chick pea and soy beans). These are delicious in quick breads.

Rice

Simmer: rice 1 part rice to 2 parts water without stirring, covering the pot

Note: Whole grain rice takes about 45 minutes to cook

Cover

Let sit: for an additional 15 minutes

Add: a little olive oil
fresh or dried herbs (parsley, thyme, cilantro, grated ginger, Bragg Liquid Aminos and sesame oil)

White Rice: has most of the nutrients removed, yet it has its place. It can be used for the 'delicate stomach', perhaps cooked with thyme or parsley

Whole Grain Rice: Some folk's digestive system can't handle the fiber of whole grain rice

Italian Rice (Arborio): is a brown or white rice that stickes to your teeth. Of course, it has to be served with grated parmesan

Jasmine Brown Rice: is a rice, white or brown, that is used with Asian foods

Basmati Rice: from India is just the best! It comes white or brown. Even the white is beneficial and far superior to the other white rice because it grows at the foothills of the Himalayas, and has a high content of minerals. Basmati cooked with a pinch of saffron is a delicacy

I heard this story once…that the mills where they remove the brown skin and bran from the Basmati rice have mounds of the 'rice polish' outside. Mothers with sick babies gather the polish, cook it up, and heal their children with it.

Sweet Rice: is sweet, therefore, cinnamon, cardamom, ginger and almonds with some lemon peel turn it into a dessert

Korean Red Rice: Cook a small amount of this with a white rice and you'll get 'purple' rice. Korean rice takes longer to cook than white rice so start it earlier. This is wonderful rice to use in stuffing Acorn or Blue Hubbard squash

Orzo: is an Italian white rice

Forbidden Rice: is a Chinese black rice which is very nourishing so you only need a little

Red Rice: can come from France (Camargue) or the Himalayas. It has a full flavor and gives your jaw a work out!

Brown Rice: This is a favorite macrobiotic rice. It comes long or short. Long grain also compliments Asian veggies

There is a fast/cleanse that some do with brown rice. For ten days eat ONLY brown rice, morning noon and evening. You can cook it mushy or drier. No spices or herbs are used. Bancha tea is permitted for a beverage. It is said that it gives rest to the internal organs. Make sure you drink plenty of water. You won't be hungry with this cleanse! Come off the cleanse by eating some steamed greens.

Wild Rice: What a treat! Cook 45 minutes to an hour until it bursts open. It tastes mighty fine with some freshly ground pepper

Some other rices are:

Bamboo Rice: (this rice is green in color because it has been dyed with the juice of bamboo leaves)

Black Japonica Rice: (red)

Red and Rose Matta Rice: Risotto is a macaroni product (wheat) that is shaped like rice.

Greens

Fresh vegetables, especially cooked dark greens, can transform your life. Nowadays, they are easily available in local grocery stores year-round, so we can be nourished by their fiber and high mineral content, even though we don't always eat them "garden fresh".

Kale, for example is full of calcium, magnesium, potassium, and vitamins A and C. The fiber and the minerals help to keep us healthy and cleanses the colon.

We are all different and have special needs, but if the food we eat is not being digested and absorbed, our digestive system will eventually become clogged and we can become sick. Constipation, for example, will prevent the toxic waste products from being eliminated from the body, and can cause problems like headaches, bloating, gas, dizziness…If the elimination problem goes unattended for longer periods illness can become grave.

To keep your food moving along, it is important to keep your colon clean. Here are some suggestions as to which vegetables would be most beneficial to you.

If you tend to be cold, and have cold hands and feet, it is best to cook your vegetables, rather than eating them raw. Eating raw foods requires more energy than eating them cooked.

During the fall and winter and into the spring, it is best to be eating some cooked foods if you live in a cold climate. In the summer, you can eat some fruit, and salads, because the temperature is already hot outside and you don't need so much internal heat.

If you are a warm blooded being with good circulation, then more raw foods are good for you. It is best to eat foods at room temperature, not chilled, because cold food slows down the digestive process.

If you are a person who has poor circulation and tends to be constipated, and perhaps "spacey," choose the vegetables that grow under the earth...the roots...carrots, beets, parsnips, burdock including them in a routine, along with some dark greens (kale, collards, swiss chard, mustard greens).

If you have good circulation, and tend to be a bit on the slow, heavy, and oily side, then you will do best by choosing celery, cabbage, and peppers, along with the dark leafy greens (kale, spinach, collards).

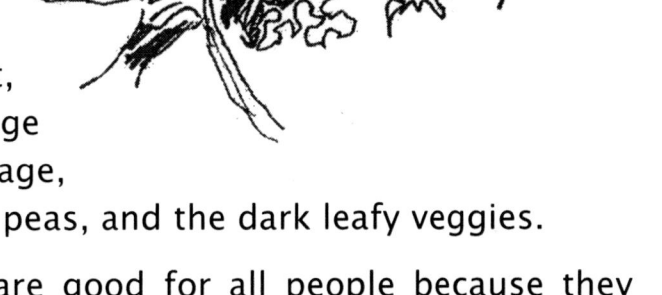

If you fall in between the two and tend to have a hot and fiery constitution, then it is best to stay away from pungent foods like garlic, onions, radishes, eggplant, and focus more on the cabbage family (red and green cabbage, Brussels sprouts, bok choy), peas, and the dark leafy veggies.

Foods like string beans are good for all people because they grow horizontally.

Ideally, if you could eat vegetables and greens twice a day along with whole grains (rice, buckwheat, millet, oats, or quinoa) and a good source of protein (red lentils, mung beans, perhaps some soaked nuts or venison), 2 Tbs. high quality oil (olive, sesame, or ghee) and some clean water, daily, you could revitalize your whole being.

Be bold. Give it a try!

Composing

I was paying $1.00 for a box of over ripe avocados at our local grocery store. The woman in front of me said, "Oh, you are going to make a lot of guacamole."

I replied, "No, these are too ripe. I am going to use them to make compost." The woman behind me said, "What is compost?" I refrained from showing my astonishment that in this rural town such a question could be posed.

So...

I explained that scrap vegetables and fruit were put into a bin or even on the earth and were alternately layered with straw or dried leaves. "This is how I make soil for the garden."

As far as I'm concerned, I cannot bear throwing a seed into the trash. It can at least be recycled if it's not planted.

Although city life may not accommodate composting, those of us with a yard or garden can. It feels good to feed the mother.

Today, in the produce isle, a young bouncy woman approached the veggies and exclaiming aloud to her boyfriend behind her "I don't want any of this organic crap. I want the real thing," as she picked up a bag of generic baby carrots...

How do people get such ideas?

How can they think that a marred carrot, not fit for sale, shaven down, called 'baby' could possibly be real?!

Artichokes

These are the easiest and most neglected delicacies in the vegetable kingdom. They are full of minerals! (iron, phosphorus, potassium, and vitamins A & C). Cooking artichokes slowly in a pressure cooker will eliminate the sweet aftertaste

Select: firm dark green artichokes

Cut: 1/2 inch off the stem

Peel: the stem

Cook: Steam in 2 inches of water until the leaves can be pulled off easily (about 45 minutes) or pressure cook for about 20 minutes

Let sit: for 10 minutes

Serving Suggestions: The way to eat artichoke is to pull off one leaf at a time, dipping the leaf in a sauce. Bite into the leaf, about 1/2 way down. Pull on it so you will be scraping the pulp off the leaf with your bottom teeth. Discard the leaf and go to the next one

Finally, as the leaves get more and more delicate, you will come to a 'fuzzy' part. Most folks cut this out or throw it away. (My Grandmother taught me to eat it.)

Then you come to the heart. You can continue to dip it into your sauce, and eat it along with the stem

Variations: Dipping sauces are easy to make

Mix olive oil, lemon, garlic, and thyme

Mix some mayonnaise with a little curry powder

Melt some butter or ghee.

Grilled Asparagus

You can braise asparagus outside on a gas grill, hibachi, camp fire, or inside in your wood stove

Cut: the white, tough ends off fresh asparagus

Drizzle: a little olive oil over the tips

Note: Brush back and forth over the asparagus with a pastry brush, painting the asparagus so that they are thinly covered with oil

Dice: some garlic

Sprinkle: garlic on the asparagus

Place: the asparagus on a grill over a campfire

or

Place: on a grill in the wood stove over red hot coals

Braise: for about a minute

Remove: from the grill

Turn: the asparagus

Return: the veggies to the fire

Cook: for another minute or so

Remove: asparagus from the coals

Sprinkle: with fresh lemon juice

Note: If you overcook asparagus, it will become floppy. The asparagus, full of moisture, tastes best when it is still crunchy

Serving suggestion: These are primo when eaten right away but are also delicious cold

Variation: Grilled asparagus are a treat over saffron basmati rice.

Beans-Refied

Heat: 2 T. olive oil in a skillet

Add: 1 chopped onion
2 cloves of garlic, minced
2 T. chili powder or cumin (or both, 1 T. of each)

Heat: until onion is translucent

Add: 2 C. cooked pinto or black beans

Mash: beans with potato masher while the beans are cooking in the aromatic oil until beans are mostly mashed

Add: water that the beans were cooked in if necessary, to add moisture

Serving suggestions: Serve on tacos or on top of Mexican rice
   Add more liquid, blending the beans and adding fresh tomatoes to make a bean dip that you can serve with freshly cut veggies

Variation: 1 tsp. powdered ginger makes a great variation if used with cumin.

Beet-Za

*If you are on a Macrobiotic, Ayurvedic, or low acid regime,
or are game for an exciting adventure, try this non-tomato 'pizza'*

Steam: in a small amount of water until soft
   2 lbs. cut carrots
   2 large beets

Blend: veggies in a blender

Add: cooking water as necessary to blend them into a thick sauce

Pour: the sauce into a pot

Add: 2 T. dried basil
   1 T. dried thyme
   1/2 t. asafoetida
   1 bay leaf

Simmer: the sauce until it becomes thick and flavorful

Adjust: seasoning to taste by adding more asafoetida or salt and freshly ground black pepper

Pre-bake: your 'pizza' dough (on next page or use quick bread dough)

Top: pre-baked 'pizza' dough with
   sauce
   oregano
   your favorite toppings (see variations)

Drizzle: a little olive oil over the top

Bake: in a pre-heated 450° oven until the crust is brown

Cut: into serving size pieces with a scissors

Variations: Toppings you can use:
   drained, crumbled tofu
   grated soy cheese
   peppers
   broccoli
   Greek olives.

Pizza Dough

Dissolve: in 1 1/2 C. warm water
        1 T. yeast
        1/4 T. agave

Beat: in 4 C. whole wheat flour
        1/2 T. salt
        2 T. olive oil

Knead: dough until it becomes elastic

Cover

Let rise: until dough doubles in size

Punch: down the dough

Roll: out dough on lightly floured surface to desired size

Note: You can make the dough thick or thin

Sprinkle: pizza pan with flour

Place: dough on a pan

Bake: until the dough forms a light crust

Remove: from oven

Garnish: with sauce and toppings

Return: to oven

Bake: until crust is brown

Variations: or make a quick bread* dough.

Tunisian Carrots

Tunisian carrots make a fine accompaniment to a Middle Eastern meal of Stuffed Grape Leaves*, Hummus* and Tabouleh*

Remove: tops of 2 lbs. carrots

Cut: carrots into 1 inch chunks

Place: in an enamel pot
carrots
1 sliced onion
4 cloves of sliced garlic

Add: water until almost covered

Add: 2 T. ground anise

Cover

Simmer: until carrots are tender

Mash: with a MOULINEX (a blender wand)

Add: just enough carrot broth to carrots to reach a mush consistency

Note: You don't want the carrots to be soupy

Squeeze: the juice of a fresh lemon over the carrots

Add: 4 cloves of diced garlic
a finely chopped bunch of cilantro
2 T. olive oil

Serving options: Serve in small portions topped with an olive
This dish is delicious reheated

Variations: These carrots freeze well.

Roasted Carrots and Potatoes

This is a very simple dish.
Make a little extra as people tend to gobble it up!

Cut: potatoes in wedges

Cut: carrots into 4 inch lengths, leaving the skins on

Put: carrots and potatoes in a bowl

Pour: enough olive oil over the veggies to give them a thin coating

Lay: veggies on a sheet cake pan

Spread: with a generous amount of
dried whole rosemary
sliced garlic

Bake: at 350° until done (about an hour),

Turn: now and then

Add: Salt and pepper to taste.

Roasting beets this way, as suggested by Naziia, is a real treat!

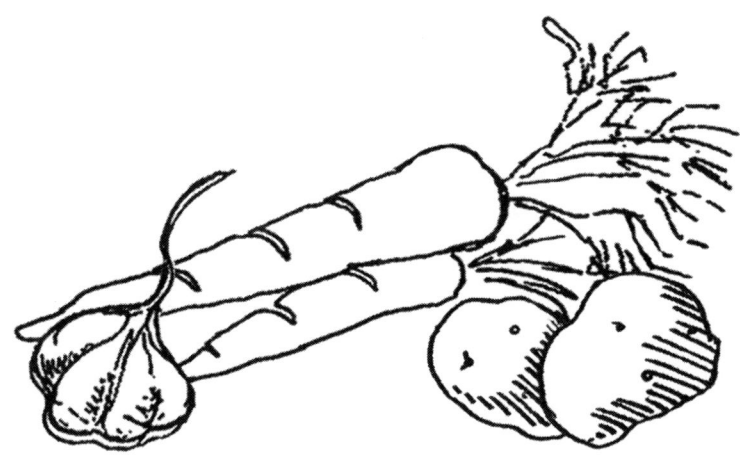

Almost Alexandro's Cactus

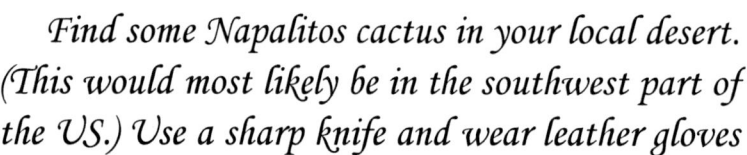

Alexandro is the Mexican man who maintains the Spa, here in Pagosa. His spirit is full of Light, laughter, kindness and talent. However, he told me he was too shy to have his recipe in this cook book. He is an integral part of my Pagosa family so I'm including the following recipe as my idea of what he would cook, knowing that Alex would pan fry, while I'm offering a water option.

Find some Napalitos cactus in your local desert. (This would most likely be in the southwest part of the US.) Use a sharp knife and wear leather gloves for the prickers, and leather boots for the reptiles. Walk respectfully, keeping your eyes and ears open.

If you are fortunate enough to wild harvest, remember to first look for the grandmother or grandfather plant in the area. Make a tobacco offering to it. Take a pinch of tobacco, hold it up to the sky and ask the elder plant where you can pick. Let the tobacco fall to the earth. Thank the plant then look around to see where you have been directed.

Pick only what you need, in gratitude. When you are finished harvesting, thank the grandmother/grandfather plant in joy and appreciation.

Depending on the season, the Napalitos may bear fruit called TUNAS. You can peel and eat these. They are filled with seeds and are juicy.

or

When in season, purchase the cactus from the produce section of your grocery store.

To Make Almost Alexandro's Cactus

Remove: the spines from 4 cactus leaves carefully with a knife

Note: If you've picked the cactus, only use the smaller leaves

Scrape: the leaves

Cut: the leaves into 1/2 inch slices

Slice: 1 onion
1 bell pepper

Chop: 6 cloves of garlic

Add: 1/2 t. chipotle powder

Place: veggies in a frying pan

Cover

Cook: in a little bit of water until tender (10 to 15 minutes)

Remove: veggies from water

Add: 1/2 bunch of cilantro chopped
2 T. olive oil
1 chopped fresh tomato

Serving suggestion: Serve with a rice mixed with soy Parmesan cheese

Variation: Instead of using a bell pepper, add 3 or 4 chopped, prepared green chilies during the last couple of minutes of cooking.

Couscous

A Moroccan wheat specialty

One New Year's Eve I had the privilege of being in Nice, France. My cousin Christine and I didn't want to party so I invited her out for couscous. In an older part of the city, we walked into a Moroccan restaurant. The tables were small, each covered with a starched pink cloth. There was one waiter. He asked me, as he seated us, if I had come to flirt with him. The three of us laughed and my American part spoke. "Non, on est venu pour du couscous." (No, we came for couscous.)

There was a row of tables on each side of a path to the kitchen which was doorless. There, stood 'grandma', the cook…the waiter's mother. She was in her slippers. What a contrast with the sparkling wine glasses, silverware, and linens!

At one point I asked Romeo how his mom made couscous. He told me that there was a secret…"Put olive oil on your hands and rub the couscous, covering each grain. Then steam it and just before serving, steam it again." What a gift he was!

Couscous comes in many forms: whole wheat, regular, large, and traditional. You can find the grain part of couscous in health food stores and in the ethnic aisle of most grocery stores.

Couscous is very forgiving. You can use Romeo's technique, putting the couscous in cheese cloth in a pot with holes in it (a steamer), or you can cover the plain couscous with boiling water, letting it puff up.

The second part of a couscous dish is the 'soup' that you pour over it. Each person is served a heaping portion of couscous. A well in the center of the couscous is made for the 'soup' ladled into it.

What constitutes the couscous 'soup' are the vegetables, the chick peas and the spices…Harissa,* You can purchase Harissa in powder form, in a tube, or in a jar. Better yet, mix your own spices.

Soup for Couscous

Brown: in olive oil
    1 chopped onion
    4 diced carrots
    2 sliced celery stalks
    1 chopped bell pepper
    4 chunked zucchini
    4 cloves of garlic chopped

Add: the juice of a lemon
chili powder (or soaked dried chiles) to taste (Choose your chiles for taste and degree of heat)

Add: packaged Harrisa or the dry powder mixture (below) to the veggies

Stir: over the heat for a minute

Add: water to cover 2/3 of the veggies
cooked chick peas (optional)

Simmer: until veggies are soft

Serving suggestion: Serve "soup" on top of couscous.

Garlic
Carrot
Onions
Tomatoes
Zuccini

Harissa

There is no specific recipe for Harissa. Everyone makes it to their own taste. You can make Harissa beforehand, storing it in a glass jar in a cool, dark place

Roast: lightly in a cast iron skillet 2 parts caraway seeds
    1 part cumin seeds
    1 part coriander seeds

Note: Some add tomato paste to the herbs

Grind: the roasted seeds

Combine: seeds with enough olive oil to make a thick, dry paste.

Egg Fu-less Yung

Melt: 2 T. coconut oil gently in an enamel frying pan

Add: one medium sliced onion
4 cloves sliced garlic
1 stalk chopped celery
1 sliced carrot
1/4 chopped bell pepper
1/2 bunch cilantro, chopped
1 baby bok choy, sliced
2 or 3 C. broccoli fleurettes
2 T. freshly ground ginger

Cook: gently

Prepare: 6 large free-range eggs (one-by-one tap them with a knife 1/3 of the way up (narrow end up) all around. Place the pointed end of the knife into the shell and cut around the top so as to remove the top, keeping the bottom 2/3 intact

Empty: the eggs into a blender or bowl

Note: Save the bottom of the eggshells (See suggestion for use on the next page)

Beat: eggs until frothy

Add: a few snow peas to cooked veggies

Warm: 2 T. sesame oil in a second frying pan until warm (not smoky)

Pour: 1/2 of the beaten eggs into sesame oil

Cook: eggs until the bottom begins to cook

Add: the veggies to the eggs

Pour: remaining eggs on top of the veggies

Cook: covered until the edges of the eggs begin to solidify

Cut: egg mixture into 4 portions

Flip: each portion in the pan

Note: You may need to add a little more coconut oil if the pan is dry to prevent sticking

Cover

Continue to cook: eggs and veggies over low heat until eggs are firm

Serving suggestion: When the eggs are cooked, serve with a drizzle of sesame oil and Bragg Liquid Aminos

Serve with jasmine rice and jasmine tea.

Eggshell Pots

Fill the bottom of the eggshells with fine sand and seedling starter mix. Use these as seedling starter pots.

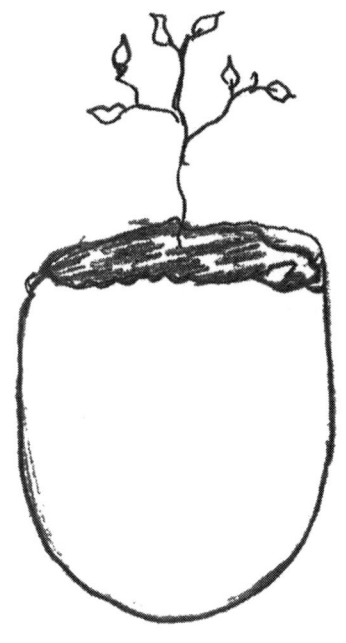

Middle East Eggplant

Slice: 3 firm eggplants in half lengthwise
Sprinkle: with a small amount of salt
Let sit: face up for 1/2 hour
Note: My French grandmother insisted on doing this to remove the 'poisons'
Rinse: the 'poison droplets' off
Peel: eggplant
Dice: into 1 inch cubes
Cover: the bottom of a large enamel pot with olive oil
Add: 1 diced onion
1 T. cumin
diced eggplant (not to worry, this will cook down)
6 sliced garlic cloves
4 more T. cumin
1 T. coriander
1 t. cardamom
Brown: mixture
Pour: 2 C. water over the eggplant
Simmer: covered for 1 hour
Stir: with a rice paddle
Add: 1 C. water
Simmer: for another 1/2 hour

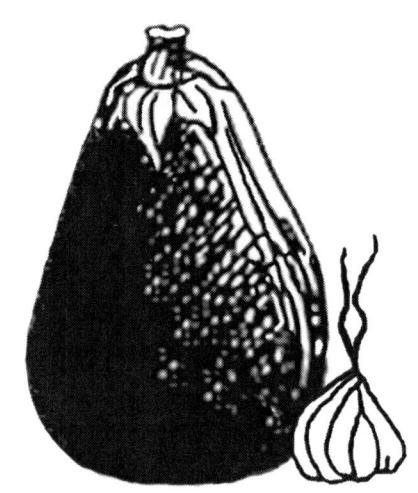

Drizzle: over eggplant a mixture of olive oil
juice of 1/2 lemon
4 to 6 minced cloves of garlic
1/2 bunch of chopped cilantro
salt to taste
Serving suggestion: Serve with basmati rice and saffron tea
 If you freeze this, wait until reheating the eggplant to add the olive oil, garlic, lemon juice and cilantro.

Felafel

Felafel, a middle Eastern delight, is usually deep fried and served inside pita bread with a sesame sauce. Here's a baked, delicate version

Soak: 3/4 C. garbanzo or fava dried beans overnight

Cook: in water until tender

Strain: 1 1/2 C. cooked beans

Mash: the beans with a wooden mallet or put them through a grinder

Add: 2 T. finely chopped onion
2 cloves minced garlic
2 T. parsley, finely chopped
1 t. coriander powder
1 t. cumin powder
1 pinch of salt
freshly ground pepper
1 t. olive oil

Mix: all the ingredients together

Divide: mixture into 8 equal-size pieces

Shape: each piece into a 1 inch ball

Place: felafels on parchment paper

Bake: at 350° for 40 minutes

Turn: felafels twice while baking

Serving suggestions: Serve with tahini
Serve with sesame dressing* and tabouleh*.

Fresh Fennel

Fennel has a delicate licorice flavor. It is stalky, resembling a celery, with wispy tops. Once you're brave enough to try it. It could become a favorite summer specialty

Cut: fennel into slices

Steam: for 15 minutes

Serving Suggestions: Serving warm with millet, rice or quinoa

Serve with a topping made with sautéed onions in olive oil, garlic and thyme

Add fresh raw tomatoes just before serving.

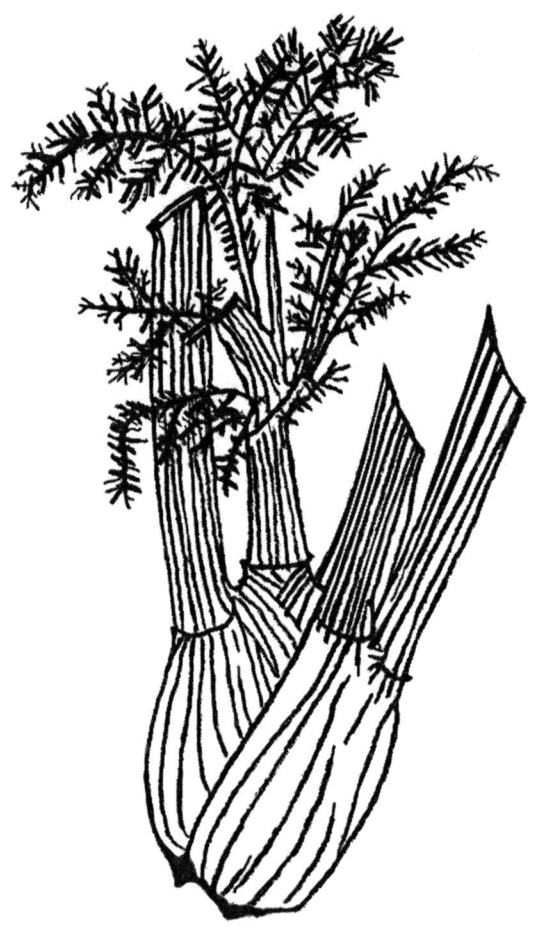

Green Chili

When Sha:nta and I moved to Colorado, we were on a tight budget. Coming from the east coast, we were fascinated by the aroma and process of roasting chilies. So, very proudly, I said to my fourteen year old, "We don't have to pay for roasting chilies; we can go home and do it ourselves!" So I bought half a bushel of chilies and put them in the oven.

Oven heat didn't do anything, so we wound up roasting them over the burners of the stove. I knew we had to get the skins off, so we proceeded to rub them and pull them off with our hands. The skins didn't come off easily so it took a very long time.

Then we began to notice, about 1/2 way through, that our hands were getting hot, really hot. Eventually we realized that it wasn't from the heat of the fire but that these chilies were HOT. Our hands were burning. Wiping them off on a towel didn't work. Washing with soap and water didn't help. Putting lotion or aloe on didn't help. Actually our hands kept getting hotter and burning more. Finally we held onto some cans of frozen juice concentrate. It took hours to calm down the burning red fingers!

Then I learned…when buying chilies there are three temperatures…mild, medium, and hot (although boxes are often mismarked!) People who sell chilies include the roasting charge in the price. After they roast them for about 20 minutes, they put them in a black plastic bag to sweat for at least an hour. This means that the skins will slip off easily! I now wear non-latex gloves for removing the skins and most of the seeds.

Most people throw the chilies in baggies and freeze them. I found that too much of the flavor is lost in the freezer, so I can them. Once you have prepared chilies you can make a 'stew' combining them with onion, garlic, carrots and zucchini.

Guacamole Tostada

Spread: a 1/2 inch layer of guacamole on a sprouted grain tortilla

Note: You can use Avocado Dressing*

Add: a layer of finely shredded lettuce
a teaspoon of salsa

Top: with shredded Soyakaas mozzarella 'cheese'.

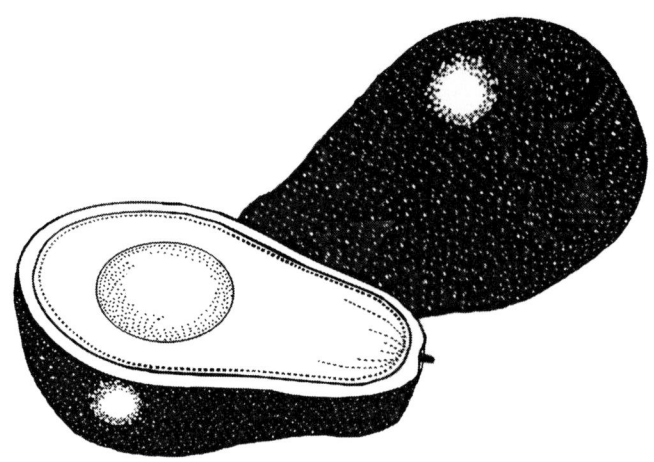

Gnocchi

Gnocchi brings back memories of my grandmother Graine. She lived in the French Alps in Valberg, a ski town. Some of my favorite childhood memories come from visiting her there.

When I was little, my ingenious mom would skimp on our food allowance, putting away a small amount every week for 5 years. Our 1st trip to France was memorable. First, there was the 19 hour flight. My mom, brother, sister and I shared 3 seats. There was always one of us lying on the floor. In exhaustion we made it to a great aunt's apartment in Paris. All I can remember is putting my head down in the plate to smell the pasta, and I was down and out for the night, in the bowl!

The next memorable French impression was to be standing out on the metal balcony watching all the bicyclists (few autos) in the street, and having a group of army guys throw some American chewing gum up to me!

Eventually, we made it from Paris to Valberg, where I was given my 1st Opinel, a French pocket knife. It had a safety lock. It was understood that I'd cut myself a few times and that's how I'd learn to use it...to carve tiny boats from pine bark. I still carry one with me as do all my cousins and their children.

So Graine, in Valberg, would mix potatoes and flour and push pieces off the fork to make these funny shaped Italian treats.

Making Gnocchi

Boil: 4 potatoes in water to cover

Peel: potatoes when cool enough to handle

Mash: or whip them until they are smooth with 4 T. olive oil

Add: 1 C. whole wheat flour

Note: Gnocchi will hold together better if you add 2 eggs but you can make them without. The dough will need to be stiff, so add a little more flour

Add: 1 t. salt
some freshly ground pepper
2 T. diced basil (optional)

Flour: your fingers

Shape: a ball out of a teaspoon of this dough

Elongate: the ball

Roll: the ball off a floured fork

Note: The gnocchi will have an indescribable curled shape with fork marks on the inside

Boil: the gnocchi about 10 minutes in water

Serving suggestions: Serve gnocchi with olive oil, garlic and fresh parsley

Serve with pesto, with or without grated gruyère or non-dairy cheese.

Kebobs

Kebobs are fun for guests to put together.
Bowls of food and stainless skewers can be put out for the grand assembly

Here are some ideas:

Marinate: cubed eggplant and firm tofu in Bragg Liquid Aminos,
      fresh ginger
      lemon
      sesame oil

Offer separately: cherry tomatoes
      red, green, orange, yellow peppers, quartered
      small onions or onion pieces
      chunks of zucchini or beets

Grill: over a low fire on a campfire or on an outside barbecue

Paint: olive oil over the kebobs as they cook

Serving suggestion: Serve with rosemary rice and a tossed salad.

Leeks

Not many folks in the U.S. eat this delicacy, although it is
a favorite dish of the French

Trim: the white ends off 4 leeks
Slice: leeks in half lengthwise
Rinse: thoroughly
Trim: the green ends so that the leeks lie flat in a 9" X 12" pyrex dish
Add: a little water to the bottom of the pan
Cover: loosely with parchment paper
Bake: at 350° until tender (30-45 minutes)
Serving Suggestion: Serve with olive oil, salt and pepper
      Serve with rice or millet with garbanzo beans and a tossed salad.

Mexican Rice

Heat: 2 T. olive oil

Add: 1 diced onion
2 cloves crushed garlic
1 green or red pepper, chopped
2 T. chili powder

Cook: on medium high heat until the veggies are browned on the edges

Add: 4 C. cooked brown rice

Sauté: with the vegetables

Add: 1 chopped tomato

Reduce heat

Cover: rice to keep warm

Serving suggestion: Serve warm with a garnish of thinly sliced scallions

Variation: To complete this protein, serve with refried beans.

Asian Noodles

Boil: rice noodles or wheat spaghetti

Rinse: in cold water

Strain: off the water

Drizzle: tahini over the noodles

Add: Bragg Liquid Aminos – to taste
minced garlic
chopped green onion (the green part)
toasted sesame oil
cayenne
tofu boiled and mashed (optional)

Mix

Taste: adjusting so that you can taste all the ingredients without any of them being overpowering

Serving Suggestion: Serve warm or cold.

Nori Rolls

Purchase: roasted seaweed from any Asian market (It is also available in health food stores but tends to be pricey there)

Note: If you can't find 'roasted' Nori, then before you use it, place each slice over an open flame of your stove top, removing it quickly. You'll see the seaweed turn green and somewhat translucent. (*Yakinori Tukusen by Takaokaya* is a brand you can look for. It comes in flat sheets, about 7 inches square)

Cook: STICKY rice until tender. (Prepare rice using twice the amount of water as rice)

Note: You can find sticky rice in the Asian market. It is also known as sushi rice

Add: a pinch of turmeric to the water to make the rice saffron color

Cool: cooked rice (you can use rice while it is still warm)

Lay: a sheet of Nori on a linen towel or on a special bamboo mat

Place: 1/2 C. of the cooked rice across the sheet of Nori and 1/3 from the bottom

Dent: the rice lengthwise with the side of a chopstick or your finger. The rice should go from one edge of the Nori to the other

Place: a piece of thinly sliced (lengthwise) cucumber in the dent or channel

Layer: cucumber with

thinly sliced avocado

thinly sliced carrots

Sprinkle: with crushed sesame seeds and sesame oil (toasted or hot)

Top: with thinly sliced ginger and a little Bragg Liquid Aminos

Roll: Nori into a roll using the towel or bamboo mat to get you started

Note: You want the rice to wrap around the veggies in a tight roll

Moisten: 1/4 inch of the end of the Nori with water so that it will seal when you have finished rolling it, taking care not to tear the Nori

Note: The Nori will get soft and elastic as it sets

Cut: the Nori roll (after it has set) in half or straight across the roll in 1 inch slices with a wet serrated knife

Serving suggestions: Serve face up as is, or with wasabi.

The 1 inch slices make wonderful appetizers

Mix wasabi powder with a little water to form a paste. It is hot like Chinese mustard.

Oatmeal

Many folks eat a bowl of oatmeal for supper. Rather than eating it sweet, here's another option. Be brave and try it before you say "ugh!"

Simmer: thick rolled oats (not instant oatmeal) for 20 minutes, until the flakes become soft

Scoop: oatmeal into a wooden bowl

Sprinkle: grated Parmesan cheese or non-dairy cheese on it

Serving Suggestion: Eat this with a small wooden spoon

Variation: Add some Bragg Liquid Aminos with a little olive oil.

Guaranteed! You'll feel satisfied

Stuffed Peppers

Cut: off the tops and center seeds of green or red peppers

Place: a small amount of water in a baking dish

Bake: at 350° until the peppers are tender (20-30 minutes)

Fill: with one of the fillings listed below

Bake: another 15 minutes

Serving suggestion: Before serving pour olive oil over the grain mixture

Variations: You can use any of these fillings or a combination:

Any kind of cooked rice with nuts, piñon, seeds, celery, parsley, rosemary, thyme, basil oregano, shallots, onions, garlic, chili powder, curry powder, coconut, quinoa, wheat berries, buckwheat, millet, orzo with jalapeños, soy parmesan, chestnuts, or tofu.

Baked Potato Party

*This makes for a fun and easy pot luck
You bake the potatoes…and your guests bring the toppings*

Toppings you can suggest:

- Homemade salsa*

- Guacamole*

- Babaganouche*

- Roasted garlic with olive oil and rosemary

- Assorted chopped veggies such as parsley, chives red onions, peppers, black olives

- Shredded almond cheese

- Green Chili*

- Tahini Salad Dressing*

- Steamed broccoli with olive oil, garlic, lemon thyme and rosemary

- Ratatouille*

- Grilled veggies such as eggplant, peppers and onions

- Harissa* (see Couscous*).

"Quiche"

This crustless "quiche" is quick and easy to make. And if you are prone to allergies, or find that milk tends to clog up your system, then you'll be happy to have this recipe as an alternative

Beat: 6 eggs

Add: 2 C. water
1 T. dried basil
1/2 t. salt and pepper

Grease: 8 inch round glass or ceramic pie pan

Cut: into small pieces
1 onion
2 cloves of garlic
1/2 broccoli
1/2 green or red bell pepper

Place: veggie mixture in a pie dish

Pour: egg mixture carefully over the vegetables

Top: with chopped chives or scallions and thyme

Bake: at 350° until the egg mixture is solid (about 20 minutes)

Serving suggestion: Serve hot or cold.

Ratatouille

Born in the heart of Southern France, this vegetable 'stew' is most tasty and is best eaten during the summer. (If you are prone to arthritis, these nightshade veggies are not for you, but you can certainly help in the picking and preparation and enjoy the full aroma that will fill the air, as it is simmering)

Cut: 1 medium eggplant in half
Sprinkle: with salt
Place: eggplant skin side down on a towel for 1/2 hour
Sauté: 4 diced potatoes in olive oil
Sauté: 4 sliced zucchini in olive oil
Sauté: 6 diced tomatoes in olive oil
Heat: 3 T. olive oil in a frying pan
Saute: until translucent
1 large onion, diced
6 cloves of garlic, diced
Cube: eggplant in 1 inch pieces (with skin)
Add: eggplant to onion mixture
Cook: eggplant mixture in frypan until the edges turn brown
Note: You may have to keep adding oil when pan frying eggplant to keep veggies from sticking
Place: sautéed veggies into a large enamel baking dish
Add: 1 T. basil
1/2 T. thyme
1/2 t. oregano
1 bay leaf
1/2 C. oil cured olives
Bake: at 350° until the potatoes are soft
Season: with salt and cayenne
Serving suggestion: Serve with grated cheese and a salad
Variation: Add cooked chickpeas for additional flavor and protein.

Salmon

*Choose frozen or fresh wild caught Pacific salmon.
It should not smell, except for having a sea smell*

Marinate: salmon for an hour in
> Bragg Liquid Aminos diluted with water
> grated ginger
> garlic
> sliced onions

Lay: salmon on a large sheet of parchment paper

Cover: the salmon with
> sliced onion
> garlic
> fresh ginger

Bring: up the 4 corners of the parchment and twist the corners so that the parchment is 'tied' on top. (There will be 4 air slots)

Place: parchment package in a pyrex pan

Bake: at 350° until the salmon flakes but isn't dry

Serving suggestions: Serve with lemon juice and chopped cilantro, wild rice and steamed broccoli

Variation: You can also steam salmon by placing it on a piece of parchment paper which you then set into a bamboo steamer.

Salmon-2

Make: a tea with
2 T. coriander seeds
1 bay leaf
1/2 t. mustard seeds
1/2 t. dill
2 whole cloves
1/2 t. dried red chile
1/4 t. salt
2 C. water

Pour: tea with all the ingredients into the bottom of an enamel pan

Add: sliced onion and garlic

Place: fresh or frozen salmon in the tea

Cover: with a sheet of parchment paper

Bake: at 350° until the fish breaks apart

Serving Suggestion: Serve with lemon juice and a sprinkle of cayenne.

Shepherd's Pie

Simmer: 1 1/2 C. (brown/green) lentils
2 /2 C. water or vegetable stock
1 diced onion
2 cloves garlic, minced
2 carrots, chopped
1/2 bunch of parsley, chopped
pinch of salt
1 t. cumin

Cook: until lentils are soft and thick

Boil: 1 lb. potatoes until tender (you can leave the skins on)

Whip: boiled potatoes
1/2 C. potato broth
2 T. oil or butter
2 T. chives

Oil: 8" X 8" pyrex pan into which you'll pour the thick lentils

Spoon: mashed potatoes over the lentil mixture

Top: with sesame seeds and thyme

Bake: at 375° for 20 minutes

Serving Suggestion: Sprinkle some rice parmesan over the potatoes before serving.

Squash Puff

This is an easy way to use leftover baked acorn or blue hubbard squash. It is even worth cooking the squash just for this subtle tasting treat

Cut: an acorn squash in half

Scoop: out the seeds

Place: the two halves cut-side down in a glass pan

Add: 1/4 inch water to bottom of pan

Bake: at 350° until the inside squash is soft (about 40 minutes)

Scoop: out the squash so that you have 2 cups

Bring: 6 eggs t0 room temperature

Beat: eggs until they are light

Add: squash
1 clove minced garlic
1/2 chopped onion
1/4 t. freshly ground nutmeg
1 C. water

Pour: the batter into a greased pyrex glass 8" X 8" pan

Bake: at 350° until the puff is firm (about 20 minutes)

Serving suggestion: Cut clean squares and serve hot with steamed vegetable greens.

String Beans

My mother's sister, Lucile, Lulu for short, believed in cooking vegetables to death so they'd be "digestible". (Never attempt to enlighten a French person because it's futile!) However, Lucile's string beans melted in our mouths. You don't have to begin where she did, but it could help!

First, Lucile lived in southern France. She and her family grew an organic garden. One summer I helped her harvest and was mortified. Lulu threw to the dirt, with vengeance, the string beans, one by one, that had dared to grow larger than a matchstick! After we picked these "French" string beans, we canned them in glass jars over an outdoor, oak wood fire. Lucile stored them in a walnut armoire upside down and used the older ones first.

Step 2. Tante Lucile (as I called her) would then heat some olive oil (from the olives of their farm) with lots of chopped garlic, which most likely did not come from China. She would open the "bocal", throwing out the juice (with all the minerals!) to simmer the literal 'string' beans in an enamel pot...for hours!!! Although this family was not vegetarian, there were never any of these haricots verts left over.

You can make your own version with our inferior beans! by steaming FRESH green beans, then slow cooking them with Italian olive oil and farmers market garlic for 1/2 hour in enamel pot. My family cringes when I sprinkle lemon juice over mine just before serving, so I learned to be discrete in order to avoid the "but that's not French" comments. (Remember to snip off the plant end of the bean before cooking.)

Tofu

Tofu is made from soy beans and is easily available in most grocery and health food stores. Asian markets may have fresh tofu. It is a most versatile food because of its neutral taste. You can add herbs, spices or sweetness to it. Tofu will pick up taste and color easily. Because it is already cooked it can be heated for a few minutes to become the protein part of your meal. Here are a few suggestions.

Tofu comes in soft, firm and extra firm. It comes refrigerated and in sterilized unrefrigerated packages. It also comes sprouted which gives it a soy bean taste. Use all varieties of tofu in soups. Use soft tofu in salads. Use firm tofu for lasagna and kabobs.

Asian Tofu

Slice: 1 lb. firm tofu into 1/2 inch slices

Marinate: tofu for an hour in
Bragg Liquid Aminos
shredded ginger
chopped garlic

Baste: with olive oil

Grill

Serving suggestion: Serve with the leftover basting sauce and fresh lemon.

Tofu Burgers-1
This is a great way to use leftover grains.
These are a hit with children and can be cooked on a grill

- **Mix:** equal portions of
  cooked grain (rice)
  tofu drained and crumbled
- **Add:** 1 egg (or egg substitute*) for every 2 cups of your mixture
- **Add:** your favorite herbs (thyme, basil, garlic)
- **Shape:** into patties
- **Pan fry:** patties on both sides
- **Serving suggestion:** Serve in a whole wheat roll with sprouts and tomato slices
- **Variation:** Grill patties.

Tofu Kabobs

- **Make:** a marinade with
  Bragg Liquid Aminos
  freshly grated ginger
  diced garlic
  a bit of water
- **Chunk:** peppers
  onions
  carrots
- **Marinade:** veggies for a couple of hours along with firm tofu, cubed
- **Place:** veggies and tofu on skewers with cherry tomatoes
- **Broil:** or braise on a grill
- **Baste:** kabobs with some sesame or olive oil
- **Serving suggestion:** Serve over rice.

Tofu Lasagna

Substitute: tofu for the ricotta in your favorite lasagna recipe

Add: 1 egg per pound to drained, crumbled, tofu

Add: parsley
thyme
basil
garlic (chopped)

Variation: For non-dairy Lasagna, use soy cheese (Soykaas) or almond or rice cheese instead of dairy

For vegetarian Lasagna, add a few roasted walnuts to the tomato sauce instead of meat

For a delightful change, try whole wheat or artichoke lasagna noodles. Gently par boil noodles so they stay intact

The egg is not crucial if you want to make a vegan lasagna.

Tofu and Rice

Cube: tofu

Add: to Mexican and curried rice dishes.

Pan Fried Tofu

When you are pan frying tofu, experiment with the size and shapes. You can make squares, cubes, rectangles and triangles. You can make long or short pieces or even shred it

Pan fry: 1/4 inch slices of tofu on both sides with 2 cloves garlic in 2 T. sesame oil. It's now ready to eat!

or

Pan fry: in 2 T. sesame oil
- 1 clove of garlic
- 1/2 red pepper
- 1 stalk chopped celery
- 1 T. fresh ginger

Add: cubed tofu

Cook: until tofu is brown

Add: juice of 1/2 lemon
a dash of Braggs

Serving Suggestion: Serve over rice.

or

Stir fry: in 2 T. oil
- 1 onion
- 1/2 red pepper
- 1 clove of garlic
- thyme
- basil
- fresh parsley

Add: cubed tofu

Sauté: until tofu is brown.

Tofu Salad
This salad is great for sandwiches

Boil: 1 lb. firm tofu for 5 minutes

Squeeze: water out of tofu

Crumble

Add: 1/2 grated carrot
1/2 stalk sliced celery
1 sliced scallion (or chives)
1/3 t. turmeric
1 t. Bragg Liquid Aminos
pinch of cayenne
olive oil to make a moist salad.

Tofu in Cold Salads
You can add tofu cubes to green salads

Cube: tofu

Boil: 5 minutes

Drain: off water

Marinate: cubes for 10 minutes in
- olive oil
- lemon juice
- thyme
- basil
- rosemary
- diced garlic
- salt
- cayenne

Serving suggestion: Toss tofu on your greens.

Tofu in Soups

Add: cubed tofu to vegetable soups

Variation: cut tofu into squares, then in half on the diagonal to make triangles.

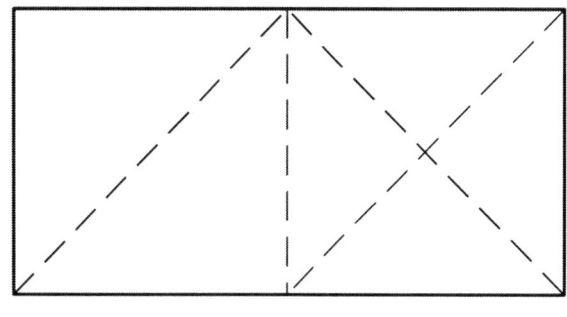

Tofu Spread

Boil: 1 lb. boiled, soft tofu

Squeeze: out water and crumble

Mix in: 1/4 C. tahini (sesame butter)
1 T. freshly grated ginger
Bragg Liquid Aminos
3 cloves minced garlic
fresh ground pepper to taste

Serving Suggestion: Use spread on crackers or in celery stalks.

Stuffing with Tofu

Par-bake: green or red bell peppers

Mash: tofu

Mix: tofu with
thyme
basil
garlic
chopped onions
oregano
salt
cayenne

Half fill: peppers with tofu mixture

Bake: at 350° until the peppers are tender

Add: a little olive oil
fresh lemon
chopped parsley

Variation: When you stuff a Blue Hubbard squash, add some cubed tofu.

Tofu Crustless Pie

Pan fry: 3 T. olive oil
    1 stalk celery
    1 chopped onion
    1 C. broccoli fleurettes
    1/4 bell pepper
    3 cloves garlic

Remove: from heat

Squeeze: water out of 1 lb. mashed, firm tofu

Add: 1 T. thyme
    1 T. basil
    1 T. oregano
    4 T. chopped fresh parsley
    4 T. Bragg Liquid Aminos
    1 1/2 T. arrowroot powder

Oil: a pyrex pie pan with olive oil

Place: tofu mixture into a greased pie pan

Mold: into a dense dome

Bake: at 350° until the top is almost brown (about 1/2 hour)

Cool: tofu pie for 20 minutes

Serving suggestion: Cut into pie slices. Eat as is or with tahini sauce

Variations: Add 1 C. cooked jasmine rice to the tofu before baking. Make sure the pie doesn't brown because then the rice will be hard

    If you eat eggs, add 2 to the tofu mixture which will make it hold its shape without having to cool first.

Pretty Good Tofu

Pan fry: 1 medium chopped onion

Add: 4 chopped garlic cloves
2 C. roasted green chiles cut into 2 inch pieces (home canned or frozen)
1 lb. drained, cubed firm tofu
6 T. chopped fresh basil or 4 T. pesto
a dash of Bragg Liquid Aminos

Serving suggestion: Serve over rice.

Tofu Spinach Walnut Loaf

Sauté: 1 1/2 C. diced onion in 2 T. olive oil

Add: 3 large diced cloves of garlic
Mix: 1 C. ground walnuts
2 lbs. chopped spinach
1 T. Bragg Liquid Aminos
1/2 lb. mashed tofu
1 1/2 C. cooked grain (quinoa, millet, rice)
a pinch of cayenne
1/4 t. nutmeg

Add: sautéed onions and garlic
Place: in greased pyrex loaf pan
Bake: at 350° for 1 hour
Heat: 2 T. butter or olive oil
Stir In: 2 T. flour
1 1/2 C. water (gradually)
1 T. horseradish
1 t. Bragg Liquid Aminos

Cook: over low heat until sauce thickens

Serving suggestion: Serve sauce over the loaf.

Tofu Stuffed Romas

Cut: 5 large ripe Roma tomatoes lengthwise

Scoop: out centers, chopping them and saving the juice

Pre-bake: tomatoes, open side up, for 10 minutes at 350° in a pyrex dish

Crumble: one box soft tofu in a bowl

Add:
- 1 T. basil
- 1 T. thyme
- 1 T. oregano
- 2 T. finely chopped fresh parsley
- 1/2 chopped onion
- 2 cloves finely chopped garlic
- a pinch of salt
- pepper

Fill: pre-baked tomato halves with tofu mixture

Cover: tops of each stuffed tomato with a large piece of onion (one skin thick)

Note: The onion will prevent the tofu from drying out and you won't have to use foil

Bake: at 350° until the tomatoes have reduced somewhat (about 40 minutes)

Serving suggestion: Serve hot or cold with a little olive oil over the top.

Wok Cooking

Choose a stainless, not aluminum wok. A copper bottom is a bonus. Instead of putting oil in the bottom of the wok use 1 C. water...then you won't be heating the oil, which is not as healthy

Place: 1 C. water in the bottom of a wok

Add: grated ginger
some cinnamon
anise powder

Arrange: veggies in layers beginning with the ones that take longest to cook

Heat: with the cover off for crunchier veggies

Add: at the last minute the top leaves of the bok choy or Chinese cabbage and snow peas

Serving suggestion: Serve with olive or sesame oil, lemon juice and Bragg Liquid Aminos over rice or rice noodles

Warm ginger tea will be a complement, along with a simple vase and a flower

Serving this meal in Asian bowls with chop sticks and Asian tea cups really adds to your creation

Variations: You might use sliced onion, celery, carrots, peppers, the white part of bok choy or Chinese cabbage, zucchini, tofu, shredded cabbage (red and/or green) broccoli, almonds, garlic, and shredded ginger

For added flavor and nutrition add some soaked and boiled until tender, lotus root (good for the heart) and dried, soaked lilies

If you want a thick sauce as you would find in a Chinese restaurant, use the following recipe.

Thick Sauce

Pour: the juice from the bottom of the wok into a pot

Mix: 1/4 C. cold water
4 T. arrowroot powder

Add: to the veggie broth

Simmer: until sauce becomes clear

Add: Bragg Liquid Aminos
lemon juice
more garlic
sesame oil

Pour: sauce over the wok veggies and stir.

Vegetable Fried Rice

With this, you will have created a nutritious dish which contains complete protein, complex carbohydrates, and assorted vitamins and minerals Bravo!

Heat: 2 T. sesame or coconut oil in a pan or wok

Add: 1 finely chopped large onion
1 stalk celery, chopped
1 green or red pepper, chopped
2 C. shredded cabbage
1 peeled, chopped broccoli stalk
1 shredded carrot
1 lb. cubed, drained tofu
1 T. shredded ginger
2 minced cloves garlic

Cook: until the vegetables are tender, stirring occasionally

Add: 4 C. cooked brown or jasmine rice
1 C. broccoli tops
1/8 C. Bragg Liquid Aminos
1 T. sesame seeds

Stir: rice mixture on medium heat, then reduce heat

Cook: covered until the broccoli is cooked but still crisp

Add: fresh mung bean sprouts

Stir and serve.

Vegetable-Rice Casserole

Brown: 1 chopped onion
2 cloves diced garlic
1 chopped carrot
1/2 chopped celery stalk
1 peeled, chopped broccoli stalk with top
1 green or red pepper, diced
1/2 lb. cubed, firm tofu
1 T. basil
1 T. thyme
1/4 C. fresh parsley
4 to 6 C. cooked rice

Pour: into a greased 8" X 8" pyrex pan

Sprinkle: sesame seeds on top

Cover

Bake: at 350° for 1/2 hour

Variation: This casserole is also good if you make a roux with garlic, onions and herbs, pouring it on top before baking.

Veggie Burgers

*You can make burgers from a protein base and/or from grains.
They are quick and easy to make and are a great way to use leftovers*

Tofu Burgers-2

Drain: 1 lb. of firm tofu

Mash: the tofu

Add: 1 egg (or egg substitute*)
1 minced clove of garlic
a few sprigs of chopped parsley
a pinch of curry powder (optional)
salt and cayenne

Add: enough whole wheat flour to make mixture hold together

Shape: into burgers

Pan fry: in olive oil turning occasionally until brown on both sides.

TVP Burgers
Texturized Vegetable Protein

Soak: 2 C. of TVP in enough water to cover it until it softens

Squeeze: out the excess water

Add: 1 egg (or egg substitute*)
garlic
parsley
thyme
whole wheat flour to hold it together
finely chopped veggies
salt and pepper

Shape: into burgers

Pan fry: in olive oil turning occasionally until brown on both sides.

Grain Burgers

Select: a cooked grain (millet, rice, and/or kasha)

Mix with protein, (tofu, TVP, seeds, ground nuts, lentils)
leftover veggies (carrots, broccoli, celery, peppers, etc.)

Add: fresh parsley
minced garlic
thyme
oregano
basil
salt and pepper

Add: an egg or two (or egg substitute*)
whole wheat flour

Note: the mixture should hold together

Shape: into burgers

Pan fry: in olive oil with garlic

Season: with Bragg Liquid Aminos

Top: with a slice of tomato and soy cheese

Variation: For grilling, add more flour to make burgers dryer.

Wraps

*Ezekiel sprouted grain tortillas come in two sizes for wraps.
These are wonderful to get you off yeasted breads*

Lay: a tortilla flat

Add: some or all of the following ingredients:
- lettuce
- cilantro
- peppers
- sprouts
- ginger
- avocado
- lemon juice
- olive oil
- green onion
- garlic
- cayenne
- cucumbers
- tomatoes or steamed vegetables with Bragg Liquid Aminos, ginger and sesame oil
- jicama
- shredded carrots

Roll: the wrap and secure with a bamboo skewer

Variations: Spread a layer of hummus, babaganouche, mashed beans or a non-peanut nut butter

You can also make wraps by using large romaine leaves instead of tortillas. Remove some of the white stem so it will roll up easily.

Asian Wrap

Lettuce, cilantro, rice or mung bean noodles, carrots, cucumber, sesame oil, garlic, ginger, Bragg Liquid Aminos and green onions.

Middle Eastern Wrap

Babaganouche or hummus, sprouts, carrots, parsley, cilantro, lemon olive oil, and cayenne.

Green Wrap

Lettuce, carrots, cucumber, celery, spinach, soaked pumpkin seeds,** green pepper, lemon, olive oil, salt, pepper, garlic, and onions.

Steamed Wrap

Steam: kale, collards, or broccoli in small pieces

Drizzle: with tahini

Add: lemon juice, fresh ginger, garlic and Bragg Liquid Aminos.

Shredded Wrap

Shred: red cabbage, carrots, and beets

Slice: celery thinly

Sprinkle: with caraway seed

Add: lemon juice, sesame oil and Bragg Liquid Aminos and garlic.

Italian Wrap

Romaine lettuce, tomatoes, parsley, pine nuts, olive oil, garlic, lemon juice, thyme, and oregano.

French Wrap

Baby greens, fresh basil, soaked hazelnut pieces,** garlic, olive oil, lemon juice, thyme, oil cured olives, and diced fresh tomato.

Spanish Wrap

Guacamole, or avocado, pico de gallo, lettuce, chili powder, and shredded rice cheese.

**Soak seeds and nuts in water the night before in order to release the enzyme inhibitors before adding to the wraps.

Baked Yams

French people cringe when you tell them about sweet potatoes or yams and marshmallows. I think they'd cringe at this too!

I've chosen yams because the inside color is more vibrant than sweet potatoes and yams tend to be sweeter than sweet potatoes

Cut: slits about every inch along the yam,

Note: make sure you don't sever the pieces, so that the yam stays intact

Place: 2 cranberries in every other slit

Place: a prepared (skinned/roasted) chile pepper in the other slits

Drizzle: with olive oil

Place: directly on baking rack or in a pan

Bake: at 350° until the yam is tender

Serving suggestion: For Thanksgiving, when there is so much food, people can break off a portion to enjoy.

Baked Large Zucchini

Sometimes zucchini seems to get away from the farmer and one morning they are 2 feet long! If you can get to the farmer's market, scoop a few of these up for winter. Store them in a cool place in your house, not touching each other or they will rot. Aging these will toughen up the skin. I like to wait until after the winter solstice to eat these, to remind me of the growing season

Slice: the zucchini lengthwise

Scrape: out the seed area with a metal spoon

Slice: some garlic and onions

Place: them along the center of the zucchini

Put: the 'boats' in an enamel pan or just on the oven racks

Bake: at 350°, for at least an hour

Note: When you insert a knife into the center the pulp should be soft

Variation: Stuff baked zucchini with herb rice before serving.

Shredded Zucchini

You can make this with any amount of zucchini. Thin to medium sized ones work best because the skins are tender

Grate: 4 zucchini

Note: Hold them from the stem side so you can grate the entire vegetable

Cover: the bottom of a glass or enamel frying pan with a small amount of water or olive oil

Put: the grated zucchini in the pan with two sliced cloves of garlic

Cover: the zucchini

Cook: until "al dente" or soft

Strain: pressing the zucchini broth through the strainer

Catch: the run-off

Add: another clove of garlic diced

Drizzle: olive oil over the zucchini

Add: freshly chopped basil

Pour: the run-off broth in to a mug to sip with your supper

Serving suggestion: The flavor of this simple dish will amaze you. Even more, if you eat this in a wooden bowl that hasn't been lacquered (this could be a 'Vermont bowl', or one you've oiled) the taste of the wood blends in perfectly. Your kidneys will also appreciate the cleanse.

Sauces for Veggies

Agave – Mustard Sauce

Brown: 1 clove diced garlic in 3 T. olive oil

Add: 1 C. water
2 T. agave
2 T. mustard
2 T. fresh parsley

Pour: sauce over cooked veggies

Garnish: with toasted or soaked sunflower seeds.

Aioli
Making this French sauce for vegetables is like making mayonnaise

Beat: 2 egg yolks (at room temperature)

Add: VERY SLOWLY in a stream,
1 C. olive oil (while continuing to beat the egg yolks)

Add: 2 t. fresh lemon juice
4 finely chopped cloves of garlic
salt and pepper.

Bragg Liquid Aminos-Ginger Sauce

Mix: 1/2 C. Bragg Liquid Aminos
1/2 C. water
2 T. grated ginger
1 minced garlic clove
juice of 1/2 lemon.

Cashew-Ginger Sauce

Blend: 2 C. toasted cashews in a blender with
3 C. water
1 T. fresh ginger
2 T. Bragg Liquid Aminos liquid amino acids

Make: a roux by heating
3 T. butter or oil, slowly stirring in
3 T. flour

Add: the cashew mixture slowly

Stir: over low heat until thickened

Serving suggestion: Serve over string beans or broccoli or your favorite veggies.

Cold Sauce

Mix: together
1 C. yogurt
1 T. thyme
2 T. dill
1 T. basil
1 T. Bragg Liquid Aminos
salt
pinch of cayenne.

Horseradish Sauce

Make: a roux by heating
2 T. butter or oil
2 T. flour
1 1/4 C. water

Add: 1 T. fresh ginger
1 T. horseradish
1 t. cilantro
pinch of turmeric
pinch of salt.

Sweet and Sour Sauce

Heat: 1 T. butter or oil
            1 C. cider
            2 T. arrowroot powder
            1 T. tamarind
            1 T. grated ginger
            2 T. agave
            1 T. Bragg Liquid Aminos

Note: This sauce will thicken at boiling point.

Tofu-Sesame Sauce

Mix: 1 C. sesame tahini with water

Add: water slowly so that the sauce first becomes thick

Note: As you add water it will thin out again

Add: juice of 1 lemon
            2 cloves diced garlic
            pinch cayenne
            pinch salt
            a few drops of roasted sesame oil

Crush: 1/4 lb. steamed tofu

Add: tofu to the sauce

Serving suggestions: Use this sauce as a salad dressing or over hot veggies
     Pour it over a rice casserole and garnish it with sesame seeds.

Delicately Indian Recipes

Through-out the years, I have found that I am happiest when I am both student and teacher. Here I pass on to you as a teacher what I have learned from Bhagavat. I have been deeply gratified and am so thankful for his time, patience and for showing me how to prepare healthy dishes.

These recipes are arranged differently here so you can cook an entire meal, easily. They are arranged so that you have a grain, protein, and vegetable meal.

Some of the recipes have been adapted in order to appeal to our Western palate. They are flavorful and delicately spiced, rather than hot and oily. You, of course, can make them hotter by adding more black pepper, ginger or cayenne. You can experiment with using more ghee. Once you have tried these recipes, I encourage you to play, substituting different vegetables, according to what pleases your taste, what you need, and what vegetables are available to you at different times of the year.

The spices are meant to help with the food's digestion, so I have also included a list of their properties to help you choose what you may need in order to improve your health.

Introduction to Ayurvedic Cooking

In order to grasp some of the technical terms used in the following recipes, I would like to share with you a brief simplified explanation of some of the Ayurvedic ways. Ayurveda is not simple, and it takes many years of study and practice to become wise to its healing potential, yet what is found in this introduction hopefully will be beneficial to you.

According to Ayurved, (a 5,000 year old practice found in India), there are three basic constitutions. Vata, is comprised of the elements of Air + Ether: Pitta is comprised of Fire + Water: Kapha is comprised of Earth + Water. When each pair of elements combine, they result in: Vata=Air, Pitta=Fire, and Kapha=Water.

As Human Beings, we have some of each of these elements within us in different ratios. When, for instance, we have Fire as our predominant element, we say that we have a Pitta constitution.

Diseases are also classified, according to Ayurved, by their predominant element. For instance, heart burn is Pitta because of its fire component. Spaciness is a Vata derangement because there is too much Air in the head, rather than in the colon where it would be helping with digestion by moving toxins out of the body.

Foods are also classified by their elemental properties. For instance, apples and broccoli are Vata. Apples are drying to the system (having to do with the Air element). Broccoli, because it flowers above the ground, brings our energy upward. If you have a Vata constitution these foods may not be so good for you because, as like attracts like, too much air in the system can cause aggravation (i.e. dryness in the intestines). Foods that grow in a downward direction, like carrots and burdock, are helpful for Vatas because they help bring the energy down from the head.

Radishes and eggplants would not be recommended for a Pitta person, during the hot summer, or one who is suffering a Pitta disorder. These foods contain too much Fire and would aggravate a "hot headed" person. Pitta needs cooling, and can receive this from sweet fruits and vegetables like figs and peas.

Cheese or avocados would not be recommended for a Kapha person, because these foods are heavy. People with a Kapha constitution (Earth + Water) are already slow moving and heavy.

They would do better with cauliflower or leafy greens that grow upward and would help their energy move upward.

According to Ayurved, disease comes from not digesting properly. When we speak of digesting food, herbs and spices are added to the food to help this process. You see, when food is not digested, very often it is not eliminated thoroughly from the body. This results in stagnation (in the intestines and sinuses) and can cause headaches. Aim to be balanced in all three sets of elements.

Tune into yourself to discover what elements are predominant within you. Then pick what foods will help BALANCE you. Choose foods that will not cause your body to strain in the process of digestion. Look for your weak areas and use foods to rebuild those parts of you. Notice what happens to you when you eat predominantly raw foods, or cooked foods. Experiment with eating certain foods because you want to foster the plant's quality within you. (I.e., does eating sweet fruits encourage a sweet disposition in you?)

The following recipes will get you started in the direction of working with the laws of Nature, in order to become healthy and vibrant. Enjoy re-discovering the ancient ways of healing...and re-connecting with the Healer.

Properties of Herbs and Foods

Asafoetida: Helps liver to produce digestive enzymes. Grows nourishing bacteria in the flora of the intestines. Relieves gas

Beets: Contain manganese, iron, for blood cell rebuilding

Bitter Melon: Drink 1 oz. of juice in the a.m. for diabetes

Black Pepper: Use freshly ground

Broccoli: Contains calcium & beta carotene

Burdock: Grounding: for rheumatism & arthritis

Carrots: 22,000 I.U. beta carotene in 4 oz., cooked

Cinnamon: Brings out the sweetness in beans

Clove: Helps get rid of gas and helps with fat metabolism

Coriander: For balance. It helps digest food

Cumin: Relieves gas

Daikon: To increase heat and digestive enzymes; grounding. For cleansing the liver and blood. Astringent

Black radishes: Are best for Kapha

Fenugreek: Helps with mucus, good for the lungs

Garlic: Has many healing properties, it helps with gas, fighting bacteria, parasites and viruses. Eat it raw and cooked

Ghee: For the liver: cleanses & tonifies it. Produces ojas, which nourishes the heart, pituitary, and pineal glands.

Ghee
Ghee is clarified butter (made from unsalted butter)

According to Ayurved, ghee enhances (ojas) the subtle essence of all tissues. Ghee increases (Agni) the digestive fires and enzymes of the body, promotes digestion and assimilation of food. It promotes the digestive fire in the small intestine. It promotes the elemental fires in the liver which govern the transformation of food in the body. It does not clog the liver as other oils and fats can, but is said to strengthen it.

Ghee is said to be food for the bone marrow and nerve tissue and it feeds the brain. Through ojas, it gives sustenance to the fire of the mind and thus enhances intelligence and perception. As such, it is an important rejuvenative tonic for the mind, the brain, and nervous system. It helps to enhance intelligence, memory and understanding.

Ghee is said to relieve sluggish intestines and is used for detoxification and the healing of wounds, alleviating peptic ulcers and colitis. It is generally good for the eyes, nose and skin. Use ghee as you would butter, on vegetables, or as a spread or in sautéing.

Making Ghee
Ghee does not need to be refrigerated

Melt: 2 lbs. of the best unsalted butter that you can find, in a heavy enamel pot

Simmer: until the cloudy liquid turns clear. (30–45 min.) You may have to push the bubbles apart to see the clarity

Test: drop a few drops of the hot melted butter into a glass of COLD water. If it splatters, the ghee is done. Another test is that the butter will smell very good!

Strain: through several layers of cheesecloth in a sieve

Pour: into glass jars with lids. What is left on the bottom (crunchies) is said to be the cholesterol.

Burdock

I am including a description of this root because it is one of the ingredients of Vegetable Soup 2* and Veggie Stew*. Its properties are quite remarkable, and it is a plant that most of you are familiar with.

Burdock is a large plant that grows in most fields. Its leaves are dark green and furry, but its most remarkable aspect is the 1/2" inch "prickly balls" that grow on it. As children, we used to pick these and throw them at each other. They would stick especially well to woolen sweaters or long hair! These were the inspiration for Velcro!

You can dig up the roots during the spring, or in the fall.

Burdock root is a medicinal root that grows in New England and in the Southwest. It can be prepared as a tea, dried, and used in powdered form in a capsule, and it can be used in cooking.

Use Burdock for skin inflammations, rashes, colds with fevers and sore throats, edema, kidney inflammation and hypertension. Do not use Burdock if you have chronic chills.

Burdock root is said to clean the blood and lymphatics. It clears congestion and reduces swelling. It is also a tonic and rejuvenates the body. It is also good for clearing emotions like anger, aggression, and ambition. It also is helpful for arthritis.

In cooking, use Burdock root as you would carrots. You don't have to peel them, but clean them well before cutting the root into 1/2 inch slices. Add 1 root to a stew.

Yogi Tea

Yogi tea makes a wonderful aromatic holiday beverage and helps with digestion

Simmer: In 8 C. water

- 4 slices fresh ginger (1/4 inch thick)
- 4 black peppercorns
- 1 6 inch cinnamon stick
- 4 whole cloves
- 4-6 green cardamom pods (crack them open)
- 8 coriander seeds

Note: Traditionally, the tea is simmered until half the liquid remains. It is still quite delicious not cooked as long, simmered to a golden brown color

Serving suggestions: You can serve it as is or you can add some milk or soy milk and/or agave

This tea is helpful if you are cold or if you have a cold and children like it as well

You can drink some daily as a cleanser and a tonic.

Chapatis

Mix: 2 1/2 C. whole wheat flour (chapati flour is best)
3/4 C. warm water (more or less depending on your flour)
Knead: dough until it is fairly soft (10 minutes)
Note: It should feel like silk or very soft skin
Cover: the dough
Let sit: in a warm place for an hour
Roll: out the dough, on a floured surface so that you get a 2 inch diameter "snake"
Slice: the dough "snake" into 1 1/2 inch pieces
Cover: the unused dough as you work to keep it from drying out
Roll: out each piece so that it is round and very thin
Heat: a cast iron skillet on medium heat
Place: the Chapati in the skillet
Press: around the edges gently with the back of a spoon
Note: Soon you will see little bubbles appear. Quickly turn the Chapatti over, and watch for more bubbles
Turn: the Chapati over using a set of tongs to its original side
Lay: Chapati directly over a gas burner flame until the chapati puffs up
Note: If you don't have a gas stove, don't despair, you can also use a little camping burner
Turn: Chapati over quickly, keeping it on the burner for a few seconds
Remove: Chapati from flame
Cover: Chapatis with a cloth to keep them warm

Serving suggestions: Serve immediately!
Chapatis can be served plain, with ghee, or used to dunk in soup, dahl, or dips.

Dahl: Red Lentil Soup

*Red lentils are high in protein and cook up quickly.
They are heating and calm Vata*

Wash: 1 1/2 C. lentils thoroughly
Boil: on high temperature with 5 C. water
Bring: to a rolling boil
Skim: off foam after beans come to a rolling boil
Simmer: for 25 minutes until the lentils are soft
Add: Chaunce (see recipe below)

Serving Suggestions: This soup can be served in a small bowl as an appetizer
   If you want to eat it as a meal, add some kale and/or collards before serving

Variation: You can make this with mung beans as well.

Chaunce

Herbs to add to dahl-soup

Melt: 2 T. ghee or use sesame, olive or coconut oil
Add: 1/2 t. powdered ginger or finely chopped fresh ginger
1/2 t. turmeric
1 t. garam masala (next page)
a pinch of cayenne
Heat: mixture until it bubbles
Pour: mixture into the cooked lentils (success = splattering of the chaunce when it hits the dahl)
Pour: some dahl into the chaunce pot and then back into the dahl to use up all the herbs

Serving suggestion: Serve with basmati rice.

Garam Masala
Making your own curry powder

Gather together:

    75 green cardamom pods or 2 T. cardamom seeds

    (3) 3 inch cinnamon sticks

    1 T. whole cloves

    1/4 C. black peppercorns

    1/2 C. coriander

    1/2 C. cumin seeds

Remove: cardamom seeds from their pods

Crush: cinnamon sticks

Combine: all of the spices

Heat: a cast iron frying pan for 2 minutes (on medium heat)

Roast: spices until they turn brown and smell very good

Remove: spiced from the pan

Place: spices into a bowl

Grind: spices in a mortar and pestle, coffee grinder or food mill

Store: in a glass jar with a tight lid.

Cauliflower Curry

Brown: 1 large onion in ghee, sesame, coconut or olive oil

Add: 2 T. curry powder (or make your own)
　　　　4 cloves of chopped garlic
　　　　2 1/2 C. vegetable broth or water
　　　　1/2 C. shredded (unsweetened) coconut
　　　　salt to taste

Add: 1 diced carrot
　　　　1 cauliflower cut into fleurettes
　　　　1 lb. cubed tofu

Cover

Simmer: until tender

Add: just before serving
　　　　2 C. peas (fresh or frozen)
　　　　juice of one lemon
　　　　1/2 bunch chopped cilantro

Serving suggestion: Serve with basmati rice.

Basmati Rice

Because Indian Basmati rice is grown in the foothills of the Himalayas, it is very rich in minerals. Washing the rice does remove some of them, but it is so abundant in minerals that there are plenty left for proper nourishment. PLEASE, it IS important to wash this rice!

Rinse: 1 C. white Indian Basmati rice three times

Stir-fry: the rice in 2 T. melted ghee until the kernels become translucent

Add: 2 C. boiling water

Simmer: on low heat for 20 minutes

Remove: from heat

Let sit: for 20 minutes

Note: The rice is now ready to serve

Variations: Add 1/4 t. turmeric or saffron

    To vary the taste and health benefits, cook the rice with a pinch of turmeric or 2 whole cloves

Note: Basmati rice is especially good for adding moisture to the skin, and for skin rashes

    It is good for all doshas to eat this rice, although Kaphas, (those who have water retention tendencies) would do best to eat less of it than others.

Kitchari
Mung Beans & Rice

Cook: 1 C. Basmati rice in 2 C. water
Cover: the rice and bring to a rolling boil
Simmer: for 20 minutes
Remove: from heat
Let sit: for 20 minutes
Boil: 1 C. mung beans in 6 C. water until the beans break down and are thick
Cut: into small pieces
3 kale leaves
6 inches of daikon
1 beet
4 carrots
1 handful of green or wax beans
1 burdock root
Place: veggies in a pot with 2 C. water
Cook: veggies until tender and add to rice
Make: the following Chaunce and add to the veggies and rice
Melt: 2 T. ghee
Add: 2 T. freshly grated ginger
2 t. garam masala
1 t. turmeric
1/2 t. asafoetida
1 1/2 t. salt
pinch of black pepper
1/4 t. black seeds
Note: The standard proportion of rice to beans is 1 part beans to 2 parts rice. If digestion is poor, the ratio can be changed to 1 part beans to 3 parts rice

    This dish can be used, especially by Vatas, for a fast or you would eat only this until the toxins, which appear as coating on the tongue, are cleansed away.

Red Lentil and Buckwheat Kitchari

*This will make a thick, hearty stew.
It would be wonderful on a cold winter's eve*

Simmer: for about 45 minutes in a covered pot:

    1/4 C. red lentils

    1/2 C. buckwheat

    1/2 T. turmeric

    1 T. cumin

    1 t. cardamom

    1 T. coriander

    4 slices ginger root

    4 cloves garlic

    4 C. water

Let sit: covered for 20 minutes before serving

Serving suggestions: Place some kale or collard greens over the top to steam while the kitchari is sitting

    Just before serving, add the juice of 1/2 lemon, 1/2 bunch of chopped cilantro and 2 to 3 Tbs. olive oil

    Hot ginger tea is a delicious addition to this supper

Variation: You can also make a Chaunce* with the dry herbs to bring out more of the flavors of the spices.

Leafy Greens

As you can see, the energy of these greens grows up and out, except for the string beans which grow horizontally. This means that the beans are good for all people and that the others are best for when we want to bring the air energy UP

Cut: the following greens into 2 inch long pieces the width of the string beans

a handful of green string beans

3 large kale leaves chopped (cut out the center stalks)

3 peeled stalks and flowerets of broccoli

Note: Green beans are good for everyone and good for the pancreas

Heat: 2 T. ghee until melted or 1 T. olive oil or 1 T. sesame oil

Add: 1 T. grated fresh ginger

1/2 t. cumin

1/2 t. turmeric

1/2 t. fenugreek

1/4 t. asafoetida

Heat: until golden, but do not overcook

Add: to spice mixture 1 C. water

all the green veggies except the broccoli tops

Simmer: covered, until veggies are tender

Add: the broccoli tops

Cook: for 5 minutes

Add: 1/4 t. real salt

a pinch of black pepper

Serving suggestion: Serve with Indian Basmati rice.

Quick Green Veggies

This not only is a quick vegetable dish but it is especially good for Kaphas if the salt is omitted

Heat: 2 T. ghee

Add: 1 T. grated ginger
1 t. cumin
1/2 t. coriander
1/2 t. turmeric
1/4 t. hing (asafoetida)
1/4 t. fenugreek
1 box frozen peas or 1 C. fresh peas

Cook: until the peas are braised

Add: 1 C. thinly sliced broccoli stalks, peeled
1/2 C. water

Turn: up the heat

Add: 1/2 t. salt
1/8 t. black pepper
1/8 t. cayenne
1 to 2 broccoli tops

Cover: the vegetables

Simmer: for 10 minutes

Serving Suggestions: Serve with Basmati rice.

Sabzi: String Beans
Provides fire and earth

Trim: the tips off 2 handfuls of green beans

Cut: beans in half

Quarter: 3 carrots and cut into 2 inch long pieces

Cut: a 6 inch piece of daikon into similar proportions

Heat: 2 t. ghee

Add: 1 T. freshly ground ginger
1/2 t. turmeric
1/2 t. cumin
1/4 t. asafoetida
1/4 t. fennel (to counteract bitterness)
1/4 t. fenugreek

Add: cut vegetables
1/2 C. water (or just enough to cover the bottom of the pan)
1 pinch of black pepper and salt

Cook: on low heat until the carrots are tender

Serving suggestions: Serve with dahl* and Basmatti rice*.

Veggie Stew

This stew is excellent for slow digestion as the root veggies bring the (air) energy DOWN

Heat: 2 T. ghee until melted

Add: 1 generous T. freshly grated ginger
1 t. garam masala
1/2 t. cardamom
1/2 t. coriander
1/2 t. turmeric
1/2 t. cinnamon
1/2 t. asafoetida

Add: the following veggies in 1/2 inch diced pieces
6 inch piece of daikon – for digestive enzymes
1 burdock root – for rheumatism & arthritis
1 beet – for manganese, iron, blood and stamina
1 yam – for hormones and stamina
3 carrots – for beta carotene
about 1 C. water
a large pinch of real salt

Simmer: adding water only if necessary to make the stew have the consistency of salsa.

This dish is yummy!

Saffron Sweet Rice

Cook: 1 C. basmati rice in
2 C. water with
1 1/2 inches of a cinnamon stick
6 whole cloves
1/4 t. salt

Remove: rice from the heat after 20 minutes, when all the water has been absorbed

Let sit

Note: The following steps can be done while the rice is cooking

Mix: together in a small covered pot
3 T. boiling water
1/3 t. saffron

Dissolve: saffron in the water

Simmer: saffron water until saffron is dissolved

Add: to saffron water
1 t. crushed cardamom seeds
1/4 C. agave

Cook: saffron mixture for 1 minute

Heat: 2 T. ghee in a third pan

Add: to ghee
5 t. unsalted pistachios or blanched almonds
3 T. raisins

Cook: ghee until the nuts turn light brown and the raisins puff up

Pour: saffron mixture over the rice

Add: raisin and nut mixture to rice

Stir well

Serving suggestion: Serve as part of your entrée or as a dessert.

Sweet Rice

Wash: 1 C. Lundberg rice mixture (fire & earth rice)

Cook: rice in 2 1/2 C. water
  1/4 t. cinnamon
  1/8 t. turmeric

Simmer: for 40 minutes

Cook: rice until there is no more water left in the bottom of the pan

Let sit: 20 minutes

Add: 2 t. ghee or sesame oil to keep rice fluffy

Serve: with Sabzi*

Variation: Substitute the following herbs: 1/4 t. asafoetida, a pinch freshly ground black pepper
  Add pistachios, pecans and/or peas.

Halavah

Boil: 2 1/4 C. water

Add: 6 large diced dates
1/2 t. cinnamon
1/4 t. cardamom
1/8 t. clove powder
1/8 t. ginger powder
pinch of black pepper

Heat: 2 T. ghee In another pan

Add: 1/2 C. cashews
1 C. whole wheat couscous or semolina

Note: The couscous grains will turn white as you stir it in the ghee, then it will turn golden. This is the time you add it to the simmering spiced date water

Simmer: for about 15 minutes until all the water is absorbed and you get little 'volcanoes'

Raise: the heat

Add: 1/2 C. agave

Cook: the halavah until it is thick and dry, stirring frequently

Remove: from heat

Cover: the halavah

Let sit: off the heat for 15 minute

Serve: as a dessert.

Coconut Candies
This delicacy will surprise you!

Melt: 1/4 lb. ghee

Add: 1 C. chickpea flour

Stir: the chickpea flour until it turns light brown

Add: 2/3 C. unsweetened coconut
1/4 C. sliced almonds
1 C. gur or jaggery (grated)
1/2 T. maple syrup

Note: Gur is a brown sugar that comes in a block form from India. If you can't find it, then sucanat would be the closest alternative, unless you can find the Spanish piloncillo

Mix: thoroughly

Remove: the pan from the heat

Cool: until the mixture can be handled

Squeeze: a tablespoon full at a time, into round balls, with your hands

Serving suggestion: Eat within 2 to 3 days!

Sauces and Condiments

Cranberry Sauce

This is one of the easiest condiments to make, and is a good project for the guys, who up until now have been allowed in the Thanksgiving kitchen only to open the can of cranberries

Open: a package of berries

Discard: any soft or rotten berries

Cover: the berries with water

Add: grated lemon or orange rind

Boil: the berries until they burst open

Add: a couple of Tbs. of agave if you like the sauce sweeter

Pour: into a bowl lined with walnuts

Chill: before serving.

Gomasio

Gomasio is a delicious sesame salt used with many macrobiotic foods. It is easy to make and adds an extra final touch when sprinkled on salads, casseroles and vegetables

Heat: over moderate heat in a cast iron pan
10 parts unhulled sesame seeds
1 part real salt

Roast: mixture until the seeds start popping

Note: The color will turn golden brown and the aroma will begin to flower

Grind: the gomasio while it is still hot until the sesame seeds are broken but not so much that it becomes butter (use a mortar and pestle, electric blender or, better yet, a "sirubachi")

Note: A sirubachi is an oriental mortar and pestle which has grooves in the bottom

Store: in a glass jar

Serving suggestion: Sprinkle over veggies, soups, salads, and tofu.

Mango Chutney

If you can this chutney, you'll always have a special addition for your recipes

Peel: 2 ripe mangos

Cut: mangos into small chunks

Add: 2 T. fresh grated ginger
2 whole cloves
1/4 t. cardamom seeds
1 cinnamon stick (2 inches long)
1/2 C. raisins or diced currants

Cover: the bottom of the pan with water

Simmer: until the mangos are tender

Add: juice of 1/2 lemon
agave (if needed for added sweetener)

Serving suggestion: Serve with curries or on sliced apples, pears, jicama or Rice Dream.

Mayonnaise

Many years ago I made dinner for a friend. He asked me why I had bothered to make bread when it was readily available in the supermarket. With my 20 year old's arrogance I figured that if he didn't know the difference then 1. I never more would bake bread for him and 2. There was nothing to say except, "I like to".

Today, eating raw eggs is not for me, but since this is a 'Transitioning Cookbook', home-made mayonnaise is included because it is healthier and tastier than commercial varieties. Hopefully, you can kindly explain the benefits, if asked why you have home-made your mayonnaise

Beat: 2 egg yolks until they are light in color

Drizzle: 1/3 C. olive oil into the eggs as you continue to beat the mixture

Note: It should become thick

Add: the juice of 1/4 lemon
a pinch of salt

Note: This should take you 5 minutes if you use an electric beater, longer if you whisk

Serving suggestion: Use this mayonnaise right away and throw out any leftovers.

Pico de Gallo

Pico de gallo is a hot/spicy condiment from the southwest. Use it as a garnish, on top of dips or on baked potatoes. You can use it with tacos, salmon, beans, rice, broccoli, zucchini and to top thick soups

Remove: the seeds and chop
- 8 Roma tomatoes
- 2 tomatillos

Add:
- 1 bunch finely chopped cilantro
- 1/2 finely chopped red onion
- 1-2 cloves minced garlic
- 1/2 minced jalapeño pepper
- the juice of 1/2 a lemon

Mix: together

Add: salt to taste.

Tahini

Make your own sesame butter!
If you use unhulled sesame seeds you will make a
heartier tahini with a rich aftertaste

Roast: 1/2 C. white sesame seeds lightly in a cast iron skillet

Turn off: heat when the seeds start popping

Stir: seeds gently

Powder: sesame seeds in an electric coffee mill, 1/4 C. at a time (or crush the seeds in a sirubachi)

Mix: with just enough sesame oil to make a thick paste

Note: Do not add more than 1/4 cup oil

Add: real salt if you must

Store: in a glass jar

Serving suggestion: Use tahini on rice cakes, for making dips, salad dressings, over hot veggies and for making cookies

Note: As the tahini sits over time, the oil will separate to the top leaving a denser tahini. You can mix it back in or skim it off to use for your next batch of tahini.

Desserts and Breads

Recipe for Mood Swings

If you are bored with your life or have problems that you want to run away from, this should do the trick. Eat some refined sugar. If you choose chocolate, expect, in less than an hour, to feel energized with some mental acuity. After this boost you'll forget you were down...until about three hours later when, if you are a sensitive person, you'll find yourself crying for 'no reason'.

If, by chance, your hormones are out of balance then that will add to your roller coaster distraction.

If you are tired of this ride then you can stop eating sugars. Have your hormones and Candida checked. Eat soaked almonds when you get a sugar craving, go for a walk or pump iron, talk it out with a friend, or do something really nice for someone else.

Namaste

Sweeteners

Many people experiment with different sweeteners, trying to make it okay to eat sweets. For instance, they say they are eating brown sugar, so their food is now healthy! Any sugar (including fruit) mixed with a grain is poor food combining causing sugar and grains to ferment. Fermentation is not digestion. If you eat sweets for the fun of them, there is a hierarchy in terms of health

Chemical sweeteners: Chemical sweeteners are at the bottom of the list. Some of the side effects can be nasty, including cancer. Corn syrup is also unhealthy

White Sugars: Next there is a white sugar, cane or beet. In producing this white sugar, be it organic or not, it is robbed of the constituents that help digest it. So, when it is eaten, it robs the body in order to be metabolized. (On the other hand, when you eat a fresh apple the enzymes it contains are present to help the apple be digested)

Raw Sugar: "Raw sugar" has actually been cooked and refined, forming crystals. It has a little molasses added back into it. Other names for this are organic raw sugar, turbinado, demarara, and muscavado

Brown sugars: Brown sugars are made by refining the sugar and then adding some molasses (which had been refined out) back into it

Molasses: Molasses is a concentrated, extracted part of refined sugar, high in iron, containing some minerals. It has a strong flavor which works well in small amounts

Honey: Honey, although much has been written about its healing properties, is highly microbial according to Dr. R. Young. Honey should never be heated, according to the Ayurveds, as it clogs the tiny vessels in the kidneys

Maple syrup: Maple syrup sure is yummy, yet it's pricey to bake with

Stevia: Stevia is a plant that sweetens. It seems to be okay for diabetics. To me it has an aftertaste that I don't care for, so I have not included it in any recipes

Agave: Agave is made from cactus plants. It is a fructose (fruit sugar). Research is saying that it is the best sweetener for diabetics and works well in cooking. It is expensive in small containers but is more reasonable in gallons. There are opposing stories about this sweetener. Some question the purity of the syrup saying that it is cut with corn syrup and that the cactus are grown with pesticides. I suppose we live in Karmagedon. If these claims are true, it makes me ashamed to be part of a race that poisons its brothers and sisters. The agave situation has been rebutted so who knows what the truth is? See how you respond to your brand of agave. If it's not favorable, make a fruit syrup by boiling and blending raisins and dates

Gur (Jaggery): There is a sugar used in India called Gur or Jaggery. It's brown, raw and unrefined, meaning that it contains the original minerals of the cane. It tastes like real food. *When I first purchased Gur in Massachusetts I had to go to someone's home to procure it. Gur came in a 2 inch thick block. My instructions were to hit it with a hammer. The hammer only made the chunks smaller, but never powdered or crushed it. So, I took the chunks and grated them.* (Gur or Jaggery is cooked and can be made from cane or palm sugar.) Now days, Gur comes in chunks in a plastic jar! East Indian grocers will usually carry it

Piloncillo: The Mexican version of Gur is called Piloncillo. Small chunks of both of these sugars can be put in a blender or boiled down in water if the recipe calls for a liquid. The Brazilian version is called Rapadura. The Columbian name is Panela. These sugars are made by pressing the juice from the cane. The juice is cooked at low heat and is stirred. (High heat causes crystals.) These sugars contain sucrose, glucose, fructose, vitamins and minerals for their digestion. The molasses are not separated out

Sucanat: Sucanat is different because the sugar and molasses are separated, then remixed.

Apple Spice Cake

This cake is wonderful with a cream cheese frosting!

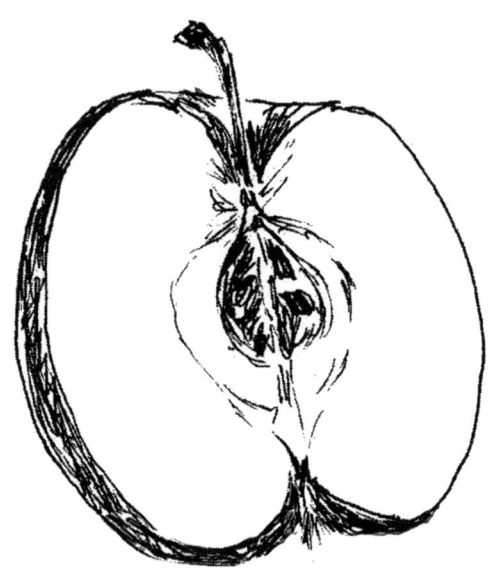

Beat: 2 eggs (or egg substitute*)

Add: 1 C. oil
1 C. agave
1 C. apple cider

Add: 4 C. whole wheat flour
1 T. baking powder
1 T. cinnamon
1/2 T. ginger

Mix Well: (The batter should be thick and almost stiff)

Add: 1/2 C. currants or raisins
2 C. apple pieces, leaving the skin on

Bake: at 350° in a greased 9 inch round cake pan for about 30 minutes

Note: When you can smell the spices for about 5 minutes, the cake should be ready

Brush: some pure maple syrup or agave over the golden brown top as it comes out of the oven.

Asparagus Bread

You might be surprised by this one. This is a unique and simply delicious quick bread. Years ago I lived in a farm-house in Whately, Mass. The house came with a huge asparagus field. We actually got sick of eating asparagus, if you can imagine that! So rather than freezing them, I tried this recipe. It worked!!! I'm hoping you'll enjoy this

Mix: 3 C. whole wheat flour
1 1/2 t. baking powder

Mix: 2 beaten eggs (or egg substitue*)
1/2 C. oil
3/4 C. agave
1/2 C. apple cider or soy milk
1/2 fresh lemon rind, grated

Blend: the two mixtures together

Add: 1 1/2 C. asparagus cut into 1/2 inch to 1 inch pieces

Pour: the batter into two greased loaf tins

Top: with walnut pieces

Place: in a cold oven

Bake: at 350° for 40–45 minutes

Remove: the breads from the oven

Drizzle: some agave over the top

Cool: the breads

Cut: with a serrated knife

Serving Suggestions: Eat as is or toasted.

Banana-Nut Cake

Mix: 4 C. whole wheat flour
1 T. baking powder
1 T. cinnamon
1/2 T. ginger
1/4 t. cloves

Make: a well in the center of the flour mixture

Add: 2 beaten eggs
1 C. agave
1/2 C. oil
1 1/2 C. apple cider or soy or hazelnut milk
1 T. vanilla

Beat well

Mix in: 4 mashed ripe bananas
1 C. walnuts
1 C. carob chip (optional)
1 C. cranberries (optional)

Pour: into 2 (8") greased pans or 1 (8") pan and a 12 muffin pan

Bake: at 350° for 25 minutes or until cake domes in the center

Variations: You can bake this cake, muffins, or bread, covering the top with granola or nuts
    You can eat it plain or add a cream cheese frosting.

Banana Cake (Eggless)

Beat: 6 T. milled, soaked flax seeds (see seeds)
1/2 C. oil or butter
1 T. vanilla
1 C. liquid (apple cider, water, or a nut or grain milk)

Add: 4 C. whole wheat flour
1 1/2 T. baking powder
1 T. cinnamon
1/2 T. ginger
1/4 t. cloves
2 C. mashed ripe organic bananas
1/2 C. chopped walnuts

Pour: into 2 8" round layer pans, greased and floured

Bake: at 350° until the edges brown (about 25 minutes)

Cool

Spread: "Just Fruit" raspberry preserves between the layers (or make your own raspberry Fruit Frosting Glaze*

Frost: with apricot gel

Decorate: with walnuts and pecans.

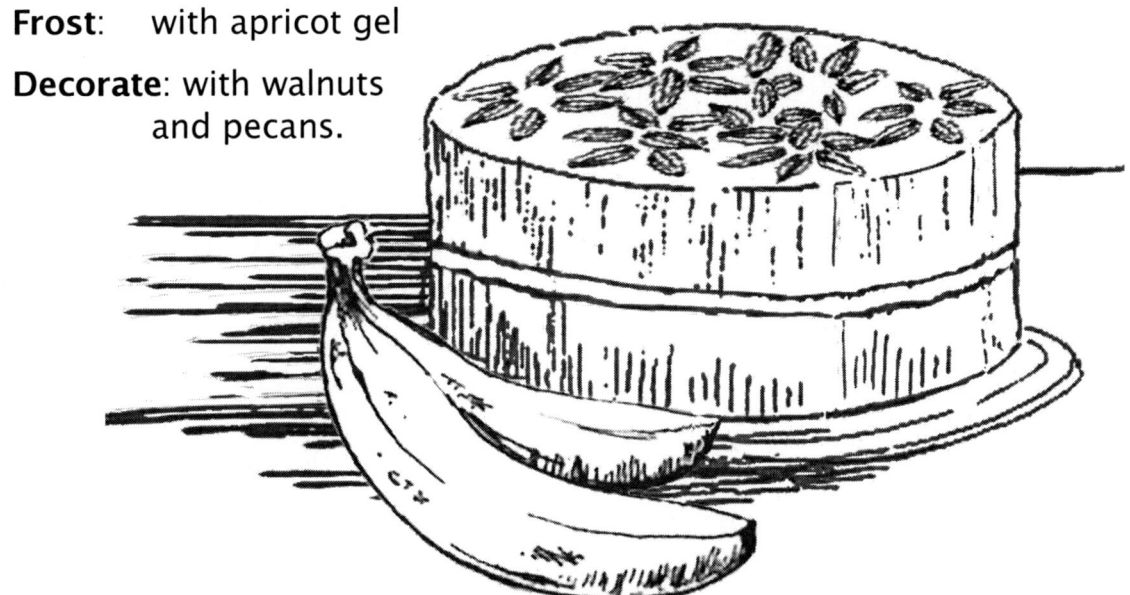

Banana-Tofu Pie
This pie is easy to make and so good warm or cold

Grease: lightly a 10" ceramic or glass pie plate

Spread: a thin layer of granola on the bottom and sides of the pie plate (about 4 cups)

Note: Don't worry if you don't get all the way up the sides, but do make sure that you cover the bottom well

Blend: in a blender at medium-high speed
1/2 cake of tofu (8 oz.)
enough fresh apple cider to be able to blend the tofu
3 ripe bananas
1 T. vanilla extract

Note: You will need about 1 1/2 cups of cider, adding it little by little as you add the bananas. Use only as much cider as you need in order to blend the mixture

Pour: the blended mixture gently into the pie crust so that the bottom of the crust keeps its shape

Note: When you get to the top of the granola, add some more granola around the edges, so you can bring the batter to the top of the plate

Slice: a banana thinly and arrange the pieces on the batter, or sprinkle some granola around the edges and dust the top with some cinnamon

Bake: at 350° in a preheated oven for 30 minutes until the center is firm when you jiggle it.

Bread

Since yeast and fermentation are not included in the alkaline way of living and eating, I want to show you how to make your own bread. You can, of course, purchase Ezekial sprouted manna or tortillas in the frozen department of your health food store

Soak: 2 C. wheat berries overnight in purified water

Throw: off the water in the morning

Rinse: the seeds

Put: the seeds in a sprouting jar or use a gallon glass jar with cheesecloth over the opening, fastened with an elastic band

Set: the jar on an incline to let extra water flow out

Cover: the jar with a towel

Repeat: rinsing evening and morning until you see a sprout as long as the seed

Grind: these seeds through a Champion juicer or food processor to make a thick, sticky dough

Note: You are not juicing the seeds

Add: 1/2 t. of cinnamon or sprouted sunflower seeds

Form: into a bread loaf

Place: the loaf on a cookie sheet covered with a piece of parchment paper

Bake: at 150° to 250° for 3 to 4 hours in your oven or solar oven

Note: This bread will be sweet and sticky with a crust.

Carob Cake

Beat: 8 T. flax seeds, powdered and soaked
2 T. oil, butter or ghee
4 T. maple syrup or agave
1 T. vanilla
1 C. nut or grain milk

Mix in: 1 1/4 C. whole wheat flour
1 C. carob powder
1/2 T. cardamom powder
1 T. baking powder

Grease: and flour an 8" round cake pan

Pour: batter into the pan

Bake: at 350° for 20 minutes

Variation: You can put this cake between 2 layers of banana cake with a "Just Raspberries" jam.

This cake is moist and is delicious as is

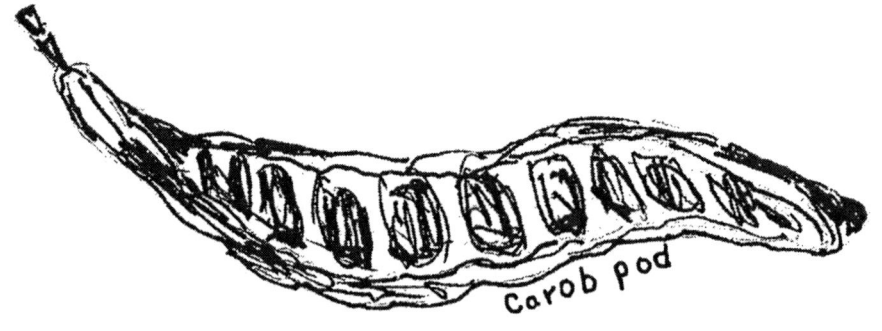

Carob-Mint Brownies

*This is a delightful way to eat wheat germ and
the minerals (especially iron) contained in the molasses!*

Mix: 1/2 C. whole wheat flour
1 1/2 C. wheat germ
1 C. carob powder
1/2 T. baking powder

Mix: 1/2 C. oil
1/4 C. agave
1/2 C. molasses
1 C. water
1/2 T. peppermint extract or a few drops of peppermint essential oil

Blend: the wet mixture into the dry

Pour: the batter into a lightly greased 8" X 8" pyrex baking dish

Top: with 1/3 C. carob chips, coconut or walnuts

Bake: in a pre-heated oven at 350° for 20 minutes or until the sides retract from the edges of the pan

Note: The outside 1/2 inch of the brownies will begin to 'crack'. The center will be moist but firm. Keep an eye on these brownies as they are better when they are moist

Cool

Cut: into serving size pieces with a serrated knife

Cover: brownies well with plastic wrap.

Carrot Cake

*This cake is delicious plain, sliced and toasted,
or with cream cheese frosting*

Beat: 8 eggs

Add: 2 C. agave
　　　　1 C. oil
　　　　1 T. vanilla

Blend well

Add: 8 C. flour
　　　　2 T. cinnamon
　　　　1 T. ginger
　　　　2 T. baking powder

Note: The batter will be fairly thick

Add: 1 lb. (6 cups) grated carrots
　　　　2 C. fresh pineapple, cut into small pieces
　　　　1 C. walnut pieces
　　　　1 C. raisins

Pour: the batter into 2 greased angel food pans (or muffin tins)

Bake: at 350° until the cracks on the muffins or cake are slightly brown and they look like they will hold their shape when removed from the oven

Note: A cake tester will come out somewhat moist.

Cherry Clafoutis

Clafouti is a French, delicate tasting dessert. Its consistency is between a pudding and a cake. If you have a subtle palate you will appreciate Clafouti

Beat: 4 egg whites until stiff and set aside

Beat: 2 egg yolks
1/2 C. agave
1 1/2 C. soy, grain or nut milk
1 T. vanilla
1 grated lemon rind

Add: 3 C. whole wheat flour

Fold in: the beaten egg whites
1 lb. fresh or frozen whole cherries

Note: The French leave the pits in the cherries

Pour: into a large oiled oval or round ceramic dish

Bake: at 350° for an hour until the top is brown

Serving suggestion: Spoon out individual portions with a large spoon

American additions: sliced almonds around the edges and/or 1/2 t. cardamom powder in the batter

Top with whipped cream on each portion at serving time.

Chocolate

If you like dark chocolate you might very well like these! If you like eating chocolate, there is a plethora of books to help you cook with it. Usually, I stay away from it because the first step in making chocolate is fermentation which is not a part of healthy alkaline eating. My preference has been to use carob, usually with a little cardamom. That chocolate is often wrapped in aluminum foil is also a drawback due to the potential of heavy metal ingestion. However, I have experimented with chocolate because I believed that some of the additives were unnecessary. Here's what you can do

Melt: Belgian baking chocolate (no sugar) in a double boiler over low heat

Note: if the chocolate's temperature rises too high it will separate and will become useless

Turn off: the heat as soon as the chocolate is almost melted

Add: a little agave

Pour: this onto parchment paper in 3 inch flat rounds

Mix: some unsweetened, shredded coconut
agave
vanilla

Spoon: 1 t. of this paste onto the warm centers

Cool

Now you have made a healthier version of chocolate!

Cranberry-Nut Bread
This Cranberry Bread freezes well

Mix: 12 C. whole wheat flour
2 T. baking powder
1 grated lemon rind
3 T. cardamom

Beat: separately
4 eggs
1 C. canola oil or 1/2 lb. butter
2 C. agave
6 C. soy, rice or nut milk
2 T. vanilla

Mix: the dry ingredients into the liquid

Fold in: 20 to 24 oz. fresh cranberries

Pour: batter into greased muffin tins or 4 loaf pans

Sprinkle: walnut or pecan pieces over the tops

Bake: at 375° until the center is almost dry

Drizzle: agave over the top as they come out of the oven.

Cranberry-Oat Cookies

You will be able to make about 30, 2 1/2 inch tasty wheat free treats!

Mix: 2 1/2 C. oat flour
           4 C. thick rolled oats

Add: 2 eggs
           1 C. oil
           1 C. agave
           1 T. vanilla extract

Blend: batter well

Add: 1/2 C. carob chips
           1 C. fresh cranberries

Place: the rather loose batter onto a baking sheet using a tablespoon

Note: These cookies will spread out a little, so leave some space between the cookies

Bake: at 350° until the edges turn brown (about 10–15 minutes).

Cranberry Oat Flour Cookies
Vegan and wheat free

Mix: 1 t. ground chia seeds
          2 T. water

Let sit: for 5 minutes

Note: The chia mixture replaces an egg

Mix: 2 C. thick rolled oats
          1 C. oat flour
          1 finely grated lemon rind
          1/4 C. canola oil or butter
          1/4 C. agave
          1 T. vanilla
          2 T. chia/water mixture
          1/2 C. small pieces of walnuts

Drop: a tablespoon of the sticky batter on a greased cookie sheet

Press: a cranberry in the center of each cookie

Bake: at 350° until the oats are brown

Remove: treats from the oven

Drizzle: agave over the top while still hot.

Cream Cheese Frosting

This frosting is delicious when you can taste the cheese, some sweetness, the vanilla, and the lemon. If one is stronger than the other, or one is not holding its own, then add slight increments of these ingredients to balance out the flavor

Beat: 1 1/2 lbs. cream cheese

Add: 1 C. agave
1 T. vanilla
1 grated lemon rind
juice of 1 lemon

Frost: With a very thin layer of frosting

Note: The icing will become 'crumby'

Frost: with a second layer of icing to give your cake a clean, creative finish

Variation: You can use orange or tangerine instead of the lemon.

Use nuts and dried fruits and fresh seasonal flowers to decorate.

Coconut Almond Bars

Mix: 3 C. whole wheat flour
5 C. thick rolled oats
3 C. coconut

Mix: 1 C. oil
1 C. agave
2 T. almond extract
1 C. fresh apple cider

Mix: together dry and wet ingredients

Add: 2 C. raisins
1 C. roasted filberts
12 oz. fresh cranberries (optional)

Note: You can easily roast the filberts by toasting them in a toaster oven until their skins begin to crinkle and you can smell their nutty aroma. Or you can pan roast them in a cast iron pan. You won't need any oil in either case. Rub the skins off in a towel

Spread: the batter evenly onto a lightly greased sheet cake pan

Mix: 8 oz. sliced almonds
1 C. coconut
1/2 C. agave
1/2 C. oil
1 t. almond extract

Spread: coconut mixture on top of the batter

Place: pan high in your oven

Bake: at 350° for 20-30 minutes until the coconut and almonds brown

Note: Some of the liquid topping may remain on the top after baking but it will be absorbed as the bars cool.

Coconut Macaroons-1

Beat: 6 egg whites until they are stiff

Add: 6 T. pure maple syrup or agave
1 T. vanilla

Stir in: 4 C. unsweetened shredded coconut
1 T. almond extract (optional or for variety)

Note: the batter will be very moist at first, but as you mix it gently the coconut will absorb the wetness. If, however, there is extra liquid, add more coconut

Dip: an ice cream scoop in hot water

Pack: the scoop with the coconut mixture so that you have a solid cookie

Place: the cookie on a cookie sheet covered with parchment paper

Note: If you are making the almond variety you can gently place an almond slice on the top of each cookie

Place: on the top tack of your oven

Bake: at 325° for 20 minutes

Note: The cookies will be ready when you notice their delectable fragrance and when they are slightly brown on the top and bottom

Remove: from the oven

Drizzle: maple syrup over the top of the cookies while they are still hot to add to their moistness.

Coconut Macaroons-2

Beat: 6 free range egg whites until stiff

Mix in: 4 C. unsulphered, unsweetened shredded coconut

Add: 1 T. vanilla
1 C. agave (according to taste)

Wet: your fingers and make 12 round compressed balls

Place: the cookies on a cookie sheet covered with parchment paper and flatten the bottoms

Note: You can use a small ice cream scoop to form the cookies

Bake: at 300° (325° for high altitude) until golden brown

Remove: from the oven

Drizzle: agave over the tops while they are still hot.

Eggless Coconut Macaroons-3
You'll be making 20 to 24 yummy macaroons

Blend: 2 T. flax seeds to a powder (see seeds)

Add: 1 1/2 C. water and blend until frothy

Mix in: 1 T. vanilla
1 t. ground cardamom
grated rind from 1/2 a lemon
4 C. unsweetened unsulphered shredded coconut
1 C. agave

Shape: 1 inch balls of the mixture, compressing the balls together

Place: on a cookie sheet or baking pan covered with parchment paper, flattening the bottoms

Bake: at 300° (325° high altitude) on the top rack of the oven until macaroons are golden brown

Drizzle: agave over the tops when they come out of the oven.

Craig's French Black Bread Bagels

Back in the 70's my brother Craig and I worked together. Originally, his recipe called for yeast. Since we are transitioning to non-fermented foods, this bread has now become a baked (not boiled) 'bagel'

Mix:
- 3/4 C. rye flour
- 1 1/2 C. whole wheat flour
- 1 T. ground caraway
- 1 t. ground fennel
- 2 T. chopped onions
- 1 T. baking powder
- 2 pinches of real salt

Add:
- 1 T. olive oil
- 1 T. molasses
- 1 1/2 C. warm water

Spoon: mixture into a greased donut baking pan

Cover: the tops with white sesame and poppy seeds

Bake: at 350° for 1/2 hour

Drizzle: olive oil over the tops as they come out of the oven.

Cécile

My French niece, who lives here and in France, just reminded me from across the ocean of what French people do when their guests arrive but dinner is late…

They (and now we!) can put out a beautiful plate, pour some olive oil on it, adding lots of finely chopped garlic, crushed salt and pepper. Then dip pieces of Craig's Black 'Bagel' (or French Bread) into the oil.

This takes less than a minute to prepare and will gather your guests around the kitchen table while you finish your dinner creation.

Crêpes

Crêpes in France can be eaten as a special afternoon snack, as a dessert or for an entire evening meal. Crêpes are festive. Crêpes differ from American pancakes in that they are thin and flat and are not eaten for breakfast. They are traditionally made with butter, milk and sugar

Beat: 4 T. powdered and soaked flax seeds
1 T. butter or oil or ghee (clarified butter)

Add: 1 C. whole wheat flour
1 1/2 C. soy, nut or grain milk
1 t. vanilla
2 t. orange blossom water (if you have it)

Rest: this mixture for an hour

Heat: a cast iron skillet, gently greasing it

Pour: a small amount of the thick liquid onto the skillet, tipping it so that the batter spreads out

Turn: the crêpe over when the bottom is lightly browned

Serving suggestion: Eat as is or they can be eaten sprinkled with agave and cinnamon or they can be filled with jam or seafood and rolled.

Date-Nut Bread

Mix: 2 1/2 C. whole wheat flour
2 t. baking powder

Beat: 2 T. flax seeds, powdered and soaked (see seeds)
1/2 C. agave
2 T. oil or butter
1 C. nut or grain milk
1/2 grated lemon rind

Mix: the dry into the liquid ingredients

Fold in: 1/2 C. walnuts or pecans

Place: 1/2 C. walnut, pecan or hazelnut pieces on top of the bread

Bake: in a greased loaf pan at 350° until the center cracks open

Remove: from oven

Drizzle: agave over the top while bread is still hot

Cool

Cut: into 1/2 inch slices with a serrated knife.

Dried Figs

The intense sun captured in these treats can transport us overseas with the first bite

Purchase: dried fruit without preservatives (Dried figs from Turkey and Greece are sweet)

Note: Avoid figs treated with sulfur dioxide, especially if you have lung sensitivities

You can eat them as is or...

Remove: the hard nubby stem

Place: figs in a glass wide mouth jar

Pour: boiling water over them to re-hydrate them in the evening

Cover: the jar and by morning they'll be plump, soft, and ready to eat

Note: Figs act like prunes so moderation is advisable

or

Remove: the hard nubby stem

Soak: the figs overnight in water

Add: the grated peel of an organic lemon

Pour: 1 C. water over the figs and lemon

Simmer: covered for 20 minutes until soft

Mash: the figs or put them through a colander

Variations: Experiment with the taste as is or

    Add some cardamom, apricot kernels or almonds to compliment the figs

    Use this fig 'jam' in between the layers of a lemon or vanilla cake instead of frosting

    You can also cook down dates with water and lemon rind to use in a similar way.

Fruit Crisp

Mix: 4 C. rolled oats
1 1/2 C. whole wheat flour
1/2 C. sesame seeds
1 C. maple syrup or agave
1/2 C. oil or butter
1/2 T. vanilla
1/2 grated lemon rind
2 C. shredded coconut

Spread: half the mixture into a greased 8" X 8" pyrex pan

Cut: into medium pieces enough fruit to make 4 Cups

Note: You can use apples, bananas, pears, peaches, whole cranberries, raisins, or blueberries

Sprinkle: the fruit with cinnamon

Spread: fruit over the oat mixture

Cover: the fruit with the remaining oat mixture

Top: with walnuts

Bake: at 350° until the top is golden brown

Remove: the fruit crisp from the oven

Drizzle: some maple syrup or agave over the top

Cool: the fruit crisp

Cut: cooled crisp into squares with a serrated knife.

Fruit Canning

Farmers markets offer us delights for all seasons. During fruit season you can 'put up' (can) for the winter. My aunt, Lucile, in France was the first to show me how she built a camp fire. She put her fruit in jars in a huge pot of water, (like an enamel corn cooking pot). She'd lay rags over the jars, then put rocks on the rags to keep the jars submerged.

Today, I follow Lucile's method in the outdoor fire pit. Two rods of rebar hold the pot above the flames. You can also cook the fruit, then pressure can them on your stove

Put: a small amount of water in the bottom of an enamel pan

Blanch: unspoiled fruit (apples, pears, apricots, etc.)

Fill: sterilized canning jars with fruit

Clean: the rim of the jars

Cap: with new lids and new or old rims

Place: the jars in a pot or pressure cooker and cover with water

Cook: according to the jar's directions (Usually boiling for 30–45 minutes)

Cool: the jars in the water

Remove: cooled jars from the water

Note: The lids need to have popped *down* for a successful canning

Store: in a dark, cool place (a pantry or closet)

Serving suggestion: Blend fruit for a cake or granola bar topping.

Fruit Frosting Glaze

Use this on top of granola bars, cakes or between layers of cakes

Mix: 2 C. blended fruit
           3 T. arrowroot powder

Note: You can use apple sauce, apricots, strawberries, pineapple, blueberries, raspberries, etc.

Heat: stirring constantly until the opaqueness turns clear

Note: The chalky consistency will melt away at the boiling point

Add: agave to taste if needed
           vanilla to taste.

You should have a thick, elastic delicious 'goo' to spread while it's still hot onto your baked dessert

Gingerbread
Non-dairy

Mix:
- 6 C. whole wheat flour
- 2 T. cinnamon
- 3 T. powdered ginger
- 1/2 t. cloves
- 2 T. baking powder
- 1/2 grated lemon

Mix:
- 1/2 C. molasses
- 1 C. agave
- 3 C. water or fresh apple cider
- 1 C. canola oil

Add: wet ingredients to dry ingredients

Pour: batter into a greased, floured sheet cake pan

Top: with thinly sliced apples

Sprinkle: with cinnamon and nutmeg

Bake: at 350° until the edges brown

Drizzle: agave over the top as it comes out of the oven

Variation: You can make this into an upside down cake by putting 1/2 C. oil or butter, 3/4 C. agave, 1/2 C. walnut pieces and crushed, fresh, drained pineapple into the bottom of the pan. Then pour the Gingerbread batter over it. After baking, let the cake cool before you turn it over.

Ginger Dunking Cookies

These cookies are meant for dunking in herb tea. They hold their shape well. Oftentimes people eat these without tea. Then, most women find them a bit strong for their palate. For men...oh my! It's as if men have finally been understood

Mix: 1 C. oil
3 C. Plantation molasses
8 C. whole wheat flour
5 T. ginger powder
3 T. cinnamon powder
1 t. clove powder

Note: Use Plantation molasses. Other molasses make the cookies too brittle

Dip: a small ice cream scoop in water

Press: some batter into the scoop

Place: batter on a cookie sheet covered with parchment paper

Press: 1 fresh cranberry into each cookie

Sprinkle: a little shredded coconut on each cookie

Place: on the top rack of your oven

Bake: at 325°-350° until the coconut turns brown

Drizzle: some agave over the top as they come out of the oven

Cool

Note: Cookies will be hard on the outside, soft on the inside.

Herb Biscuits / Bread

You can also wrap this dough around a thick green stick to be cooked over an outdoor campfire

Mix: 2 C. whole wheat flour
1 T. baking powder
1 T. thyme
1 T. basil
1 T. crushed rosemary
1 t. garlic powder
1/2 chopped onion
3 T. freshly chopped parsley
pinch of salt and pepper

Add: 1/4 C. olive oil
3/4 C. water of vegetable broth

Top: with sun flower seeds
1 T. thyme

Flour: your hands to form biscuits

Bake: at 350° on parchment paper

Variation for bread:

Grease: and flour an 8" X 8" pyrex pan

Bake: until the seeds are brown and a knife comes out cleanly

Drizzle: olive oil over the top as the bread comes out of the oven.

Hermits

Mix: 2 C. whole wheat flour
1/2 T. baking powder
1 T. cinnamon
1 T. ginger powder
1/2 t. nutmeg
pinch of cloves

Mix: 1/8 C. butter or oil
1/4 C. molasses
1/4 C. agave
6 T. water

Mix: together wet and dry ingredients

Add: 1/2 C. dried currants or raisins
5 chopped organic dried apricots
1 chopped dried pineapple slice
1/2 C. walnuts

Turn: onto a piece of parchment paper or a cookie sheet

Press: the dough out to 1/3 inch thick

Bake: at 325° until the dough is cooked but not hard or crispy (30 minutes or so)

Drizzle: agave over the top when they come out of the oven

Cut: hermits into rectangles.

Jello-2

I don't know why people like this, but they do, so I'm including it.

During the summer, I stock up on fresh strawberries, blanch and freeze them. Raspberries go to the freezer as is. So, defrost 4 cups of strawberries and one package of raspberries. Put the strawberries in the blender with a tiny amount of water if need be

Sprinkle: 2 envelopes of gelatin into 1/2 C. water (or juice)

Let sit: for a minute

Boil: 1 C. of the strawberry purée

Mix: into the gelatin

Add: the remainder of the cold purée

Add: whole raspberries

Set: this in a cold place until it begins to set

Whip: a pint of whipping cream until stiff

Note: Try to purchase heavy cream in a glass bottle

Add: 2 t. vanilla
1 T. agave

Re-whip: cream being careful not to over whip, turning it into butter

Mix: whipped cream gently into the almost set Jello

Pour: mixture into parfait glasses or into a bowl

Cover: each portion

Cool: for at least 2 hours.

Licorice Candy

Make: 1 1/2 C. anise tea with
1 T. anise seeds

Mix: in 3/4 C. molasses
1/4 C. oil

Boil: the mixture

Add: 1 T. pectin (do not soak the pectin first)

Boil: 1 minute

Add: 1 1/2 C. white flour
anise oil to taste

Roll: out into 'snakes' 3/4 inch in diameter

Cut: into 1/2 inch long pieces

Dry: on parchment paper for several weeks in a dry room

Turn: often (daily) so that the licorice dries evenly.

Olive Quick Bread
This bread calls for breaking off chunks rather than slicing

Dry roast: 1/2 C. hazelnuts gently in a cast iron skillet

Put: them in a terry cloth towel

Rub: the skins off

Crush: nuts with a mallet

Mix: 2 C. whole wheat flour
1 T. thyme
1 T. baking powder
pinch of salt
3 T. flax seeds, powdered (see seeds)

Add: 2 T. olive oil
1 C. water
3 T. chopped oil cured black olives
1/2 of the crushed hazelnuts

Grease: parchment paper

Place: parchment into an 8" layer cake pan

Form: the dough into a dome with the edges not touching the rim of the pan

Place: the remaining nuts on top of the bread

Bake: at 350° until a knife comes out almost dry

Drizzle: with olive oil as bread comes out of the oven.

Pain D'epices (Honey Bread)

Pain D'epices is a traditional French quick bread, made without oil or eggs. It keeps for a long time, if wrapped well.

In France, 4:00 is the time for the "gouter". It is the time for a snack, perhaps a cup of coffee and a pastry, but more often it consists of a piece of bread with a piece of chocolate in it, or a piece of Pain D'épices. This simply delightful bread easily tides a hungry belly over until the 8:00 evening meal

Mix: 4 C. whole wheat flour
1 T. baking powder
1 T. cinnamon
1 T. anise (powder)

Add: 1 1/2 C. honey or agave
1 1/2 C. hot water

Blend: the wet ingredients into the dry ones

Pour: the batter into a greased bread pan

Bake: at 350° for about 50 minutes until the crust is brown and the center is fairly dry

Remove: from the oven

Brush: immediately with some honey or agave over the top

Cool: the bread cool

Cut: into 1/4 inch slices with a serrated knife

Serving suggestion: Serve Pain D'epices as is, toasted, or with jam or honey

Variation: You can add 2 T. of butter and the rind of an orange to the batter.

Kato-Persimmon Bread

Beat: 3 eggs
1/2 C. oil or butter
1 C. agave
1 t. vanilla

Mix in: 4 C. whole wheat flour
1 T. baking powder
1 t. cinnamon
1 t. nutmeg
1/2 t. ginger
1/2 t. allspice
2 C. persimmon pulp
1 C. raisins
1 C. walnut pieces

Pour: into 2 or 3 greased bread loaf pans

Top: with pecan or walnut pieces

Bake: at 350° for 35-40 minutes

Drizzle: agave over the tops when coming out of the oven.

Fruit Pies

*This is a basic guideline for fruit pies so that both
the fruit and crust will be cooked*

Make: a pie crust...try the Easy Pie Crust*

Prepare: the fruit filling while the crust is pre-baking

Note: Depending on the size of your pie dish, estimate how much fruit you'll need, remembering that as fruit cooks the volume will diminish. You will need between 4-6 cups

If you are using apples, pears, fresh pitted cherries or berries:

Cover: the bottom of a pot with water

Add: fruit

Steam: the fruit until they are blanched but not soggy

Pour: the cooking liquid into a heat-proof measuring cup

Add: enough water to the cooking liquid to make 1 C. liquid

Add: 3 T. arrowroot powder
1 T. cinnamon

Return: liquid to the heat

Stir: until the opaque liquid becomes a clear syrup

Add: grated lemon rind and/or agave (optional)

Pour: syrup gently over the fruit

Pour: fruit and syrup into the pre-baked pie crust

Bake: pie at 350° for 35-40 minutes or until the fruit mixture bubbles.

Pie Crusts
Basic, old fashioned

Hand mix using a fork: 1 part cold, shredded butter
3 parts whole wheat pastry flour

Add: a few teaspoons of cold water gradually

Form: dough into a ball using your hands

Cool: dough for 1 hour covered

Roll: the dough out on a floured board

Note: The less you handle the dough the flakier it will be

Pre-bake: this crust 10 minutes before filling

Note: Pre-baking will help keep the crust from getting soggy during cooking

Variations: Add
some agave (for sweetness)
salt and sesame seeds (for entrées)
lemon rind
nut meal (pecan and hazelnut)
dried coconut.

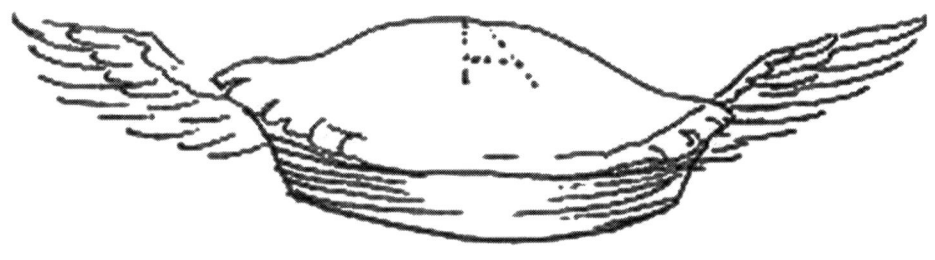

Easy Pie Crust

Line: a pie pan with a thin layer of thick rolled oats on the bottom and sides (about 3 cups)

Transfer: oats from the pie pan to a bowl

Oil: the pie pan

Add: 1 1/2 C. whole wheat pastry flour
2 T. white sesame seeds
a large handful of dried coconut
1 T. cinnamon
1/2 grated lemon rind
2 T. canola oil or melted butter
3 T. agave
2 T. cold water

Place: mixture into the greased pie pan

Bring: the oat mixture up the sides

Pre-bake: at 350° for 10 minutes

Fill: the pre-baked crust with a cooked fruit mixture (fruit cooked with agave and arrowroot powder as previously discussed)

Bake: the filled crust until it's lightly browned.

Granola Pie Crust
Here is an easy fruit pie crust you might enjoy

Choose: the pie plate you want to use
Pour: a thin layer of granola into the pie pan and add enough to cover the sides
Pour: granola into a bowl
Add: enough oil and agave or maple syrup (in equal proportions to add moisture an stickiness to the granola
1 t. of cinnamon if the granola doesn't already have some
Oil: the pie plate
Pour: the granola back into the pie plate
Spread: mixture on the bottom and up the sides
Pre-bake: the crust for 10 minutes at 350°
Heat: 8 C. of fruit on the stove (Cover the bottom of the pan with apple cider or water)
Note: Use a base of apples. You can add some blueberries, nectarines, raisins, a lemon rind or whatever fruit you have a passion for
Cook: the fruit just long enough so that they become tender but not mushy
Pour: off some of the liquid into a bowl
Cool: the liquid
Mix: in 3 T. arrowroot powder to the liquid
Add: the arrowroot mixture back into the fruit
Note: The mixture will thicken as it cooks. When cooked, the juices will become clear, rather than opaque
Spoon: the fruit gently into the granola crust
Garnish: the edges or top of the pies with either more granola or some shredded coconut
Bake: at 350° for 20–30 minutes until the granola turns brown and the fruit is nice and hot
Remove: the fruit pie from the oven
Cool: before serving.

Pineapple Upside-Down Cake

Melt: 1/8 lb. butter

Pour: melted butter into the bottom of a 9" X 12" glass pan

Add: 1/2 C. agave or maple syrup
1 freshly sliced or crushed pineapple
1/2 C. walnuts

Beat: 2 eggs

Add: 1 C. butter or oil
1 C. agave
1/2 C. molasses
2 C. apple cider

Add: 6 C. whole wheat flour
2 T. baking powder
2 T. cinnamon
2 T. ginger

Pour: the batter over the pineapple mixture

Bake: at 350° until the batter is cooked (about 30 minutes)

Remove: cake from the oven

Let sit: in pan for 10 minutes

Turn: cake upside-down onto a platter that will accommodate some of the syrup spilling down over the edges

Variation: For a more festive look, sprinkle some unsweetened coconut around the edges.

Poppyseed Cake

What has been fun is to make one cake in an angel food pan plus a dozen cup cakes or a couple of layer cakes to keep in the freezer

Heat: until almost boiling
2 C. poppyseeds
3 C. soy milk

Allow: mixture to cool while you make the rest of the cake

Beat together: 6 eggs
1 lb. butter or 2 C. oil
3 C. agave
1 T. vanilla
1 fresh lemon rind, grated

Mix: 8 C. whole wheat flour
2 T. baking powder
1 package fresh cranberries

Make: a well in the flour mixture

Pour: the liquid into the center

Blend: the egg mixture into the flour

Fold: in the poppyseed mixture

Pour: batter into 2 or 3 greased angel food pans

Top: with some granola

Bake: at 350° for 40 minutes (or until the cracks that form on the top become dry)

Variation: Add a package of fresh cranberries to the batter before baking.

Prune Tart

This is a simple tasting tart which accentuates the sweet taste of prunes

Pour: boiling water over 2 C. pitted prunes

Cool: the prunes

Drain: the dehydrated prunes, saving the juice

Tart crust

Mix:
- 2 C. whole wheat flour
- 1/3 C. butter or canola oil
- 1/4 C. agave
- 2 T. flax seeds (powdered and soaked)
- 1 to 2 T. prune 'water'
- 1 finely grated lemon rind

Grease: a large glass or ceramic pie dish

Place: the soft dough in the middle of the dish

Press: out the dough with your knuckles and fingers (or roll it out first)

Pre-bake: at 350° for 12 minutes

Mash: the prunes with an electric wand

Add: 1 T. vanilla

Note: You might need to add some of the prune juice. The prune purée should not be perfectly smooth

Spoon: the prunes into the pre-baked pie crust

Bake: at 350° for 25 minutes

Serving suggestion: Serve warm or cold in small slices.

Pumpkin Muffins

Bake: a small pumpkin

Scoop: out the cooked pumpkin pulp

Blend: with enough apple cider, nut milk or water to produce 6 cups of thick pumpkin

Beat: 4 eggs
1 C. agave
1 C. oil

Mix in: 2 C. thick rolled oats
9 C. flour
6 T. cinnamon
2 T. ginger
1/2 t. cloves
1 t. nutmeg
1 C. raisins

Add: the pumpkin purée

Scoop: batter into large greased muffin tins

Cover: with granola or nuts and coconut

Bake: at 350° until the tops burst open

Drizzle: agave over the top when muffins come out of the oven.

Pumpkin Pies

This will make several 8 inch pies depending upon whether you use eggs or not

Beat: 8 eggs

Add: 6 C. cooked pumpkin
2 T. cinnamon
1 T. ginger powder
1/2 t. cloves
1 1/2 C. agave or maple syrup
4 T. molasses
3 C. rice or almond milk

Pour: into a granola pre-baked pie crust

Bake: at 350° until the center is firm

Variation: You can also make this pumpkin pie without the eggs and liquid.

Quatres Quarts
Four quarters

This is a very old recipe. Graine, my grandmother, then later Simone, my mother, made this cake. In those days they used a scale, the kind you'd put a weight on one side and the food you wanted to weigh on the other side. All four ingredients would weigh the same (eggs, sugar, butter and flour). Today you could use a digital scale

Weigh: 4 eggs on a kitchen scale

Weigh: out the same weight in whole wheat flour (approximately 2 C.)

Weigh: out the same weight in softened butter

Note: The butter will weigh about 1/2 lb. but it's better to use 1/4 lb. otherwise it will be too rich

Beat: the eggs until light and fluffy

Beat: the butter into the eggs

Add: 1/2 C. agave (instead of sugar)

Mix: in the flour

Note: You should have a thick batter

Add: rind of 1/2 lemon
1 tsp. vanilla (if you like)

Bake: at 350° in a greased bread pan

Serving suggestion: Eat the Quatre Quart in slices as you would a pound cake.

Rice Balls

You will need to use sweet rice for this recipe because it is very sticky.
Asian markets carry sweet rice

Cook: 1 C. sweet rice in
2 C. water

Let: the rice sit for 20 minutes

Mix in: 1 T. cinnamon
1 t. cardamom powder
1 1/2 C. shredded coconut (unsweetened)
2 T. thick tahini (not too oily)
1 T. vanilla
2 T. agave
1/2 C. dried currants or tiny pieces of dates
2 T. freshly grated ginger
1/2 grated lemon rind

Drop: by tablespoons full into a bowl of shredded coconut

Roll: until you have a covered ball

Let sit: overnight in a cool place

Serving suggestion: Serve as a mid afternoon snack or as a dessert for your Asian meal.

Rice Pudding-1

Mix: 4 C. cooked brown rice
1/2 C. agave
2 T. butter or oil
1 T. vanilla
4 beaten eggs (optional)
1 freshly grated lemon rind
1 C. raisins or chopped dates
2 t. cinnamon
1/2 t. ginger
1/4 t. ground nutmeg

Pour: mixture into a greased ceramic or glass baking dish

Bake: at 325° in a preheated oven for 1 hour

Note: The pudding will thicken as it cools

Serving suggestion: Serve as is or with a dab or raspberry preserves or whipped cream...or both!!!

Rice Pudding-2
Non-dairy

Mix: 4 C. cooked brown rice
1/2 C. hazelnut milk (or soy or almond milk)
1/2 C. agave
1 T. canola oil
1 T. vanilla
1 grated lemon rind
1 C. raisins or chopped dates
1/4 C. chopped, unsulphured apricots
1/2 T. cinnamon
1/2 t. nutmeg
1 t. ginger powder

Top: with sliced almonds

Pour: into a greased pyrex pan

Bake: at 325° for 1 hour

Serving suggestion: Serve warm or cold.

Ricotta Cheese Cake

This is an old recipe adapted from my New Rochelle High School's Spanish teacher, Mrs. Grasso

Bring: all the ingredients to room temperature

Beat: until smooth:
1 lb. ricotta cheese
1 lb. cream cheese
4 eggs
1/8 lb. butter (melted)
1 C. agave
1 pint sour cream
1 t. lemon juice
1 t. vanilla
grated rind from 1 lemon
3 T. arrowroot powder

Grease: a 10" cheese cake pan

Cover: the bottom of the pan with a layer of maple granola

Pour: the cheese mixture gently into the pan (over the granola)

Place: the cake in a cold oven

Bake: for 1 hour at 350°

Note: the center should be firm

Turn off: oven

Let sit: for 2 hours in the oven

Serving suggestion: This cake is best when refrigerated overnight
 It can be eaten as is or topped with fresh blueberries or raspberries.

Sorbet

Made with fresh fruit
You will have created the healthiest creamy frozen dessert!

Freeze: overnight a bunch (about 6) organic ripe bananas with the skins on
a quart of strawberries (or use whole frozen strawberries)

Note: Don't bother using the regular, gassed bananas

Thaw: the bananas at room temperature for about 10 minutes

Peel: the bananas

Slice: bananas into 1 inch chunks

Put: bananas and frozen strawberries through a Champion juicer so that you are not juicing but passing all the fruit through the machine

Serving suggestion: Serve immediately

Variation: You can also use frozen mangos, blueberries and raspberries in the banana base.

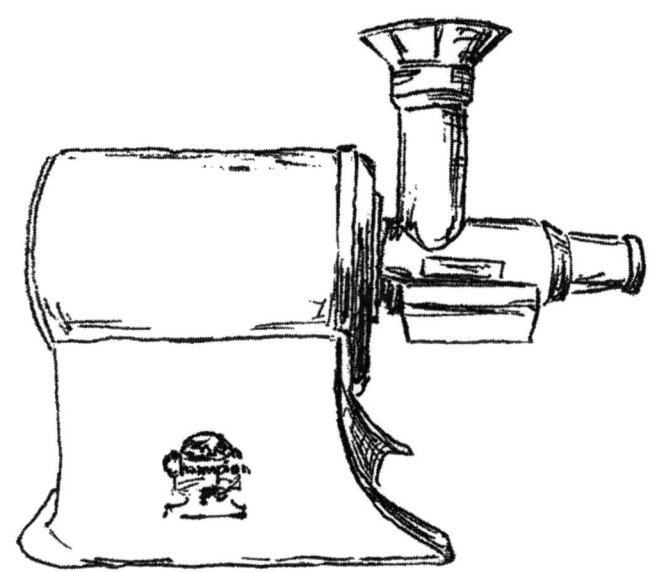

Tahini Candies

*Children love these, not only eating them, but making them!
These candies look quite decorative on a doily on a silver candy dish, piled in a pyramid*

Mix: with a wooden spoon to make a thick paste
1 C. tahini

1/2 C. sesame seeds
1 C. agave
1 C. carob powder
1 T. vanilla
1 C. currants

Add: some shredded coconut if the mixture is a bit oily

Shape: mixture into balls using a teaspoon

Roll: balls in unsweetened coconut

Note: You will need about 4 cups of coconut to roll out all of these treats

Store: in a tight container.

Tahini Cookies

Mix: 2 C. tahini or almond butter
1 C. agave
1 C. canola oil or butter
1/2 T. vanilla
4 C. whole wheat flour

Drop: by spoonfuls on parchment paper or a cookie sheet

Bake: at 325° on the TOP rack of your oven.

Vulcan Wedding Cake

This recipe belongs to Tufeen Hushami. I would change the flour to whole wheat flour, the margarine to butter and sugar to agave, 1/2 C. I'm including this recipe, not because it's alkaline but because no cookbook is complete without a Vulcan recipe. To be made as a wedding cake, many rituals would have to be performed during the making of the cake. This is a non-ritual version

Sift: 6 oz. ground almonds with 1/2 C. flour
Add: 1/2 t. salt
1/8 t. cloves
1/8 t. nutmeg
1/4 t. cinnamon
1 1/2 t. baking powder
Mix: in a separate bowl and let stand
6 oz. grated carrots
1 T. grated lemon rind
1 T. lemon juice
1 T. Vulcan bitter nectar
Note: Dark Jamaican rum may be used
Cream: 5 T. margarine
6 oz. sugar (a bit more than 3/4 C.)
Separate: 5 eggs
Beat: the yolks into the margarine and sugar mixture
Add: carrot mixture to the eggs, margarine and sugar
Beat: egg whites until soft peaks form, then set aside
Mix: the dry ingredients into the carrot mixture (batter will be thick)
Beat: the egg whites a little more
Fold: batter into the egg whites
Mix: batter gently until it is just barely evenly mixed
Pour: into a greased ring mold
Bake: at 325° for about 50 minutes or until a skewer comes out clean
Remove: from oven
Cool: for 5 minutes
Unmold: onto a serving plate dusted with confections sugar
Note: The sugar prevents the cake from sticking as much.

Wolfberry Protein Bars

Wolfberries are small, long, red dried berries found in Asian markets or health food stores. They are sometimes called lichee berries

Mix: 2 C. spelt flour
1 C. soy or chick pea flour
1 C. coconut (dried)
1 C. sesame seeds
1 C. raisins
1/4 C. wolfberries (the Asians eat wolfberries for longevity)
1 1/3 C. agave
1/2 C. tahini
1/2 C. oil
2 T. cardamom powder
3/4 C. soy or rice milk

Bake: at 350° in a 9" X 12" glass pan until the top is slightly brown

Cut: bars into squares.

These bars freeze well

Making Yogurt

Buy: a small container of PLAIN organic Greek style yogurt

Note: Stoney Farms makes some without pectin or sugar

Heat: until almost boiling, 1 quart of organic milk

Note: Milk can be 0% fat, skim milk, whole milk, or raw milk

Let cool: until the milk is at the temperature that you can put some inside you forearm, and it doesn't burn. Now it's at the right temperature for the next step (106°)

Remove: the 'skin' from top of the milk with a spoon

Place: yogurt in a bowl with 6 T. of milk

Note: This dilutes the yogurt

Mix: the diluted portion into the remaining warm quart of milk until you have a smooth texture

Decant: the yogurt and milk mixture into glasses or cups

Place: cups in a pan which is 1/2 filled with warm water

Note: Don't cover yogurt containers with water!

Cover: the yogurt containers with a glass lid

Keep: the pan and water WARM overnight

Note: You can do this in a crock pot if it doesn't get too hot or set the pan in a styrofoam cooler. 106° is a good temperature

Pour off: any water that may have separated out from the yogurt in the morning

Refrigerate: covered any yogurt you don't eat

Save: one yogurt container, without spices, to use as your starter for the next batch

Serving suggestion: Mix into the yogurt as you eat it, ground cinnamon, cardamom, cloves and coriander to help with digestion.

A Birthday Cake

One of my delights is to cook for people who have special dietary needs. For instance, people who have celiac and are on a non-gluten diet are most surprised when they are offered an amaranth cookie. Preparing vegan non-dairy meals has been a joy.

Having been invited to a birthday pot-luck party I wanted to bring a cake. Then I thought of the guests and their eating habits…In order to suit their needs, I included a card which said, "non-dairy, non-wheat, non-gluten, vegan, all natural with no calories."

What I brought was a cake in the shape of a dome, made out of snow. The candles in the snow cake were lit. Everyone laughed as it was used as a glowing centerpiece.

Bringing a birthday cake to a party can be touchy, but this one seemed to bring a smile to all.

Addendum

Coffee

In Ayurved there is a saying that all foods are good for something. This means that not all foods are always good for everyone at all times; therefore, we could benefit by being discerning and educated.

This book does not contain recipes for coffee drinks, desserts or candies because coffee is a potent medicine, to be respected.

Coffee, aside from being ACID and a fermented product, pumps up the heart and stressing the adrenal glands. Over time, it can clog up the tiny vessels in the kidneys.

As medicine, coffee is useful in a few ways. If one needs to be awake driving for a long period of time, then as one of my dear teachers, Rosalyn Bruyère suggested, drinking it only at these times allows the coffee to have its best effect.

Using coffee for cleansing the liver through colon irrigation is another medicinal use.

Two friends encouraged me to rub wet coffee grounds on my face. I tried it. Wow! What a refreshing exfolient which leaves the skin so soft…and that's all I have to say about coffee.

The Desert

Recently, I was asked to cater an outdoor ceremony that lasted five days. Northern New Mexico is beautiful but rattlesnake country. We were advised to wear thick boots at all times.

I don't know if this will help any of you, but I felt better, arriving prepared…

Because my local hospital told me that the snake serum was only available at hospitals, and we would be two hours from the nearest one, I packed a kit for those two hours.

The Medicine People talked to the creature that was enjoying the hot sun by medicine wheel. The medicine man and I went to make sure it had understood to vacate the premises. Thankfully, it did. So for five days we were watchful and it was uneventful.

This was my kit:

Camphor essential oil: for my boots to ward off snakes

Ledium: homeopathic remedy in case of bite

Belladonna: homeopathic remedy in case of a bite

Bromaline: an enzyme to ingest to eat up the venom

Salt: to put on the bite to draw out the venom

Ammonia: to put on the bite

Onion: to put on the bite

Cold ice: to put on the bite

Whisky: I'm not sure what this was for, but I imagine to calm people down. Maybe it helps with the venom?

Drying Foods

Mangos, yum! Several times a year, mangos appear in the markets

Peel: mangos and slice them uniformly

Sprinkle: fruit with fresh lemon juice

Place: fruit on a screen (not metal) or dehydrating trays

Note: It's good to have perforated trays so that the food dries from all directions

Place: the trays in a warm, dry, breezy area (a porch works well)

Turn: the mangos every few days until they are leathery

Store: in glass jars.

A Guide to Drying

Sprinkle: the following with lemon before drying: apples, cantaloupe, carrots, pears, strawberries, turnips and zucchini

Dry: as is, on the porch: blueberries, cranberries, celery, onions, raspberries, red cabbage and herbs…parsley, rosemary, peppermint, etc.

Dry: in the sun pineapple, fresh figs, apricots sprinkled with lemon

Variations: I have a fabulous stacking, hanging, fresh air dehydrator from the Food Pantrie. It has stacked trays with nylon mesh walls

You can, of course, use an electric dehydrator

Or use a rack on the top of a low fire woodstove. Lay the rack over two bricks, then place bananas sliced in 1/2 inch pieces on the rack to dehydrate

Serving suggestions: Use the dried fruit in granola or trail mix

Use the veggies to make your winter soups.

Fat Burning

If you'd like to boost your ability to metabolize fat, you can include:

Sucking on and eating whole cloves, one at a time. Cloves also tend to curb the appetite, (two or three per day).

Adding cinnamon, ginger or garlic to food is also helpful.

Grapefruit is an old standby to be used in moderation if you're aiming for an alkaline diet.

For most people eating the normal American diet, changing to alkaline foods will shed pounds quickly.

Gluten Intolerance

Some people are allergic to gluten. Not only do they need to stay completely away from gluten foods, they also need to stay away from non-gluten foods that have been cooked on gluten food surfaces. This means that if a non-gluten person orders a steak or a hamburger which has been cooked on the grill and the grill has not been thoroughly cleaned the non-gluten person can get VERY ill

Here is a list of gluten and non-gluten grains and flours

Gluten: oats, rye, spelt, kamut, graham, couscous, barley and wheat in all forms (bulgar, seitan, semolina pasta)

Non-gluten: acorn flour, amaranth, arrowroot powder, artichoke, buckwheat, chestnut, coconut, garbanzo, job's tears, kudzu, quinoa, sorghum, tapioca, taro, teff, and yucca

Cooking suggestion

Cook amaranth, buckwheat, job's tears, quinoa, and teff as you would rice

Amaranth Flour Cookies
Vegan non-gluten cookies

Mix: 1 C. amaranth flour
1/2 T. cinnamon
1/2 T. ginger
2 T. agave
1 T. canola oil
1 t. chia seeds (powdered and soaked in 2 T. water)
1 T. water of vanilla (if you want a soft cookie)
1/2 C. crushed walnut pieces
rind of 1/2 lemon, grated

Form: into flat cookies

Place: a pecan on the top of each soft cookie

Bake: at 350° on a cookie sheet covered with parchment paper

Drizzle: agave over the top when they come out of the oven.

Gluten Free Cookies
These cookies are fragile and have the consistency of sugar cookies

Mix: 1 C. non-gluten flour mix (Bob's Red Mill)
2 T. canola oil or butter
2 T. agave
1 t. baking powder
rind of 1/4 finely lemon, grated
1 t. orange blossom water
1 T. vanilla

Form: flat cookies

Place: cookies on a greased cookie sheet

Place: an almond or pecan on top of each cookie

Bake: at 350° until slightly brown.

Gluten-Free Pie Crust

Mix: 1 C. unsweetened shredded coconut
1/2 C. almond flour (mill the almonds in a coffee grinder)
2 T. coconut flour
2 T. canola oil or butter
2 T. agave
a few drops of water

Press: the mixture into an 8" pyrex pie plate

Bake: at 350° until golden brown.

Note: Do not overcook this one as burnt coconut is nasty!

Fill: with a 'Just-Fruit' jam (i.e. St Dalfour's Kumquat, or make your own variety with arrowroot powder).

Incense

*Have you ever wondered how incense is made?
It is an art that I am not purporting to be an expert at, yet I can get you started at making your own*

Gather: or buy some of the following
your native plants which have a beautiful aroma
pine pitch that has dried
piñon greens
rose petals
sandlewood bark

Note: Make sure all of your ingredients are dry

Whiz: them in a coffee mill

Note: The finer the powder, the easier the incense will burn

Strain: the powder

Re-whiz: the rougher parts

Add: an amount of Makko equal to your powder

Note: You'll have to order some Makko on-line. This is an exotic bark that will help your incense burn. I don't suggest using the chemical potassium nitrate

Add: enough water to make a dry, thick paste

Form: into cones (with wet hands) or put some on the end of a bamboo skewer

Let dry: before burning

Variations: California sage leaves are a wonderful addition to any recipe

You can also add essential oils

I like to mix some tree greens, resin, flowers and spices, for instance: cedar greens, frankincense, lavender flowers and star anise.

Low Glycemic Foods

Many people claim to be losing weight by eating low glycemic foods. This makes sense and this idea is not new. This information helps us be more aware of what we choose to eat.

Dark green veggies have always been good for us and have a low glycemic index. The sweeter veggies (beets, carrots, parsnips) have a higher rating.

If you are going to pay attention to the glycemic index, choose foods that rate 55 or less and know that 70 and higher is BAD!

What is confusing with the index is that a chocolate bar, for instance, can be in the high 40s while a rice cake is over 80 and watermelon is over 100. This might lead one to choose a chocolate bar over the fruit; processed sugar over a whole food that contains enzymes for digesting it.

Yes, low glycemic is preferable in the scheme of a healthy diet, but it's only a small piece of the nutritional puzzle.

Nightshades

The most commonly known nightshades are tomatoes, potatoes, eggplant and peppers.

To expand on these, the list includes cayenne pepper, and foods that contain nightshades...catsup, ratatouille, spaghetti sauce, babaganouche, potato salad, eggplant parmesan, Tabasco, and barbeque sauces. Potatoes with green skin are the worst, sweet potatoes and yams are not part of the nightshade family.

The problem with eating nightshades is for folks with arthritis and or muscle twitching. Nightshades are high in alkaloids which tend to cause joint pain. However, half of the alkaloids are removed by cooking nightshades.

There are a few other nightshades on the list: mandrake, goji berries and tobacco. I don't know if burning the tobacco reduces the alkaloids in cigarettes.

The name 'nightshade' has been given to these plants because they grow during the night.

Oils for Sinuses

Sinuses can be a challenge for many. The core reason, aside from structural issues, is a weak immune system that can't handle toxins...in food or the environment

A two-fold approach can be helpful:

    Build up the immune system with echinacea angustaflora root (not in a tincture) and astragalus root.

    Cut out potentially allergenic foods such as peanuts, corn, wheat, sugar, dairy and soy.

Here are two oil options:

    Using Castor oil as a base (2 oz.) add a few drops of tee tree, eucalyptus, and imortel essential oils. You should be able to feel the essential oils, but not have them burn, so begin with two drops of each. Put a few drops in a Q-tip and swab inside your nose.

    Mountain Alternatives, (706) 258-3221, makes an aromatherapy inhaler. It's a plastic tube with a hole at one end for inhaling. The fiber core can be saturated with eucalyptus, tea tree, imortel, and camphor essential oils from your health food store. Sniff these oils as needed.

Seeds

Seeds offer a good source of calcium. You can soak them (pumpkin, sunflower, flax) or roast them (sesame) or eat them whole or powdered (chia.) Three Tbs. of chia seeds have about the same amount of calcium as a glass of skim milk.

You can enjoy them on salads, in spring rolls, as sprouts and in smoothies and salad dressings. Put them on top of home-made crackers (poppy) and as a vegetable topping. Mustard seeds are delicious in East Indian foods.

Imagine the seed that goes into the ground. What strength it has to protect itself from the underworld so that it can grow into a beautiful plant or flower, providing a plethora of seeds. That's what I want in my body…to keep me strong and creating.

Using Seeds as an Egg Substitute

This egg substitute can be made by using ground, soaked flax or chia seeds

Use: 2 T. egg substitute for each egg

To make 2 Tbs. of egg substitute:
Soak 1 t. of ground seeds (flax or chia) in 2 T. water.

My appreciation goes to Tess Challis who encouraged me to experiment with using flax seeds in order to transition away from the use of eggs

Wood Stove Cooking

A mindset here in Southern Colorado is 'getting ready for winter.' We plan for winter year-round. There's what most folks do to earn a living during three seasons, then there is relying on those efforts to get through winter

So, here are some suggestions that have helped me:

1. Gather a few trash barrels of pinecones to help get the woodstove fired up.

2. Melt paraffin or used candles over a very low heat on your cooking stove. Fill one third of cardboard egg cartons (not the styroform ones) with sawdust. Pour the melted wax into each compartment. Cool and store until the days get short and cold. Break a section to light your fire. It burns much longer than paper and won't clog your chimney as pitch can.

3. Collect stainless racks which will easily fit in your woodstove. When it's time to cook, heat one on the coals, then place your olive oiled salmon or veggies on this grill. (Potatoes, you can just put into the coals in order to bake them.) Grill asparagus, zucchini, carrots, egg plant, onions and peppers.

4. The ceramic inserts from crock pots make wonderful humidifiers. Adding a few drops of an essential oil (lavender, eucalyptus, orange, tea tree) to the water and placing it on top of the wood stove will diffuse the aroma throughout your home.

5. During the winter holidays, remember chestnuts! With the point of a sharp knife, cut an X into the flat side. Place them in a long handled popcorn popper, moving them so that they don't burn. They should be ready to eat in 15 minutes.

6. This is not a cooking tip, but one that has merit. Eddie, our car mechanic and Pagosa native, told us to put some logs in the snow so that they would burn slowly and last the night. Yes! It works!

7. You can always have a pot of tea, (I use a glass coffee pot) or soup or stew, in a thick enamel pot simmering on the stove for yourself or your guests.

8. The top is a great place to warm tortillas.

9. Using an elevated rack laying on two bricks you can dehydrate vegetables and fruit on a low heat wood stove top. Bananas are delicious dehydrated!

10. Wood stoves and camp fires are ideal places to put those angry letters or 'love' letters that would best be offered to Spirit.

Effervescent Bath Balls

These are for ceremonial use only. (Just kidding!)
However, they do turn an ordinary bath into a luxury

Mix: 1 C. citric acid
           1 C. arrowroot powder
           2 C. baking soda

Mix: 1 1/3 C. oil (coconut, almond, olive, etc.)
           1 T. essential oil (lavender, eucalyptus or rosemary
           a drop or two of patchouli)

Mix: the ingredients well

Compress: the mixture with your hands into dense balls (4 inch or so in diameter)

Dry: on parchment or wax paper for a few weeks until they are dry

Turn: occasionally

Store: the Bath Balls in cellophane bags with a pretty ribbon as a gift for yourself or others

Use: the entire ball or pieces of it in your warm bath.

Equine Help

Pam called. "What do you have to help my horse's leg?"
"What's the problem?"
"A tibia fracture."
I gave her an Ayurvedic herb, manjishta,** to mix with water to apply to his leg. Along with physical therapy, the horse began walking. In 2 1/2 months he was back at full speed. Since then I came up with several oils and a salve

The following are some mixtures of oils that you can make in a base of apricot oil, which is thin and easily absorbed:

To repel flies: Apricot oil, add the essential oils of eucalyptus, cedar wood and citronella. Apply on its mane, forehead and legs but stay away from its eyes

For a stuffy nose: Check to see if the horse has worms, parasites, or mold on its hooves. In apricot oil add the essential oils of lavender, eucalyptus, camphor, and tea tree oil. Apply this on her upper lip under her nose. If she does have parasites, apply cistus essential oil along her spine where the parasites are apt to hide out. Apply bergemont oil over her intestines. Putting some colloidal silver in her clean drinking water can also help get rid of parasites. Neem oil is smelly but also effective against parasites. Neem is also an anti-inflammatory

For an achy spine: Make a mixture of apricot oil, adding castor oil and the essential oils of birch, camphor, myrrh, white thyme and geranium. Apply these daily to his spine area

For the legs: This oil is a favorite. To apricot oil, add castor oil and the essential oils of eucalyptus, white thyme, camphor and sassafras. You need only a few drops of each essential oil as they are potent and made to be diluted. Five to seven drops will suffice. If the oil is too strong for you, it's too strong for your four legged friend, so dilute it with more oil base.

To Make a Salve

To make an authentic salve, you would simmer plants, roots and flowers in oil to distill the properties you desire. Here is a simpler way.

Put: 2 T. Shea butter in a double boiler with 1 t. olive oil

Melt: 5 minutes over low heat

Allow: the oil to cool

Add: 6 drops of some or any of the following
tea tree oil
lavender essential oil
grapefruit essential oil
peppermint essential oil
white thyme essential oil
oregano essential oil

Pour: salve into a small glass cosmetic jar

Allow: to cool

Use: where you would use an antiseptic first aid cream.

My quest for finding a good source of molasses for the ginger cookies, led me to a feed store to try the molasses they feed horses. It's called molasses. The tiniest taste made me spit and wash and wash and wash out my mouth for half an hour. It was mixed with alcohol! (I suppose to keep it liquid?) I would NEVER offer this poison to any horse.

**Manjishta is an anti-inflammatory, anti-microbial herb that helps to detoxify the liver and mend bones. One tablespoon can be added to your horse's feed daily or you can mix it with water for a poultice on an injured area. Wrap the area, changing the wrap daily.

Fun Foods for Children
*The following are quick, healthy and easy foods
that most children can also make*

1. Spread rice cakes, large or small, with tahini or almond butter. (Peanut butter is out because of the fungus contained in peanuts)

2. Spread nut or seed butter on sliced apples, jicama or cucumbers

3. Top Ezekial sprouted tortilla, warmed or cold, with sliced tomatoes and shredded almond or rice cheese, with olive oil thyme and oregano

4. Soak overnight, pumpkin and sunflower seeds, or almonds, pecans, and filberts

5. Mix organic raisins or currants with soaked almonds

6. Mash and cook a banana with 1/2 t. carob and 1/2 a pinch of cardamom powder and 1/4 t. vanilla. Spread on apple or pear slices

7. Fill celery stalks with almond butter

8. Place a sliced banana in a blender. Add fresh strawberries with just enough almond milk or water to blend

9. Put fresh lemon juice and/or fresh mint in a glass of water to entice drinking more water

10. Slice cucumber, sprinkling with lemon juice and dill

11. Children can scoop out a ripe avocado, sprinkle it with lemon juice, mashing it to put on a rice cake

12. Split the top of a large date, removing the pit. Fill with nut butter or a piece of fresh pear.

Food for Teeth

Only once, when I said to my Osteopath, "I want to regrow my lost teeth" did anyone speak about nutrition for teeth. He advised me, "You'll have to increase your calcium for that."

I work with food and nutrition daily. Did I ever think to hone in on dental needs? My focus was on nerves, pain, blood, alkalinity and learning lessons. When faced with dental pain, I would put herbs and oils on my gums but the thought that teeth could be nourished from the inside never occurred to me. Now that I see the possibilities, it makes me wonder why dental professionals don't talk about food for teeth.

To be honest, I have never understood the bowl of candy for patients at dental offices. The message to me is, "Eat sugar, it keeps you coming back." Homeopathic X-ray or Arnica could be a more helpful gesture.

If you are experiencing trouble in your mouth, I hope that you will be able to glean something helpful from this chapter. This is my story and I am not prescribing anything.

Standing in front of a chiropractor friend's office, he said to his incoming patient, "Boy, you look different." She proudly replied, "Yes, I had all of my teeth pulled and I feel like a new person." There's no plug here for teeth extractions. The point is that unhealthy teeth can be the cause of seemingly unrelated problems. Ask your dentist for a handout which shows how each tooth is connected to a meridian, which in turn interfaces with each of our internal organs.

What I am about to share with you is the journey of the healing of my teeth, TMJ, and body after a car wreck which forced me to look deeper and wider. Although the following information is my experience, hopefully there will be something here that will be beneficial or healing for you and loved ones.

How many times did I hear, "Oh, TMJ, there's not much we can do to help." Or "TMJ and facial pain is a medical nightmare." Or "I don't see anything the matter with your tooth. Why do you want to have it pulled?" So, for 5 years I traveled to Phoenix and Santa Fe for help.

In Santa Fe, there was a Prosthodontist who made a very refined night guard. (Never wear an upper appliance that covers the palate because it interferes with the cranial rhythms of the head, brain and therefore the rest of the body). Each visit consisted of fitting or adjusting the night guard, then driving across town to a Craniologist. He was a French Canadian who was a learning experience in and of himself. He used to say things like, "In America, you have to be nice to people. Otherwise, they won't come to see you. So I always have to make an effort tobe nice. That's so annoying." We'd laugh, which as you know is a great healing remedy. Then back to the Prosthodontist I'd go for a check to see what the cranial session had done and to make sure that the night guard was perfectly positioned to alleviate the TMJ pressure.

When I told this dentist that a tooth was hurting, and the x-ray showed nothing, he'd put some vegetable dye on the tooth, which could show a fracture or crack. This would explain the pain. Sometimes we'd crown that tooth.

In the car accident, I'd hit my teeth on the steering wheel, broken my nose, wrecked my knees, hit my sternum and fractured my right shoulder. There were also closed head injuries. The car was totaled. For two years, I was blessed with 5 to 7 treatments each week which included Chiropractic, Rolfing, Acupuncture, Cranial Sacral work, Aromatherapy, Quantum machine therapy, Laser therapy, Hands on healing, Homeopathic treatments, Watsu, Homeopathic remedies on CDs, Magnetic therapy, and swimming 5 days a week in our warm sulfur springs.

In Phoenix, My Dentist had a Cavitat, an ultrasound-type machine used to determine the porosity of bone. The process involved putting gel on the gums, then sliding a smooth device over them in order to take pictorial readings of the bone conditioning of the upper and lower jaw. The computer printed out a multi-colored graph which depicted the varying levels of health-to-rot.

Several times I returned to My Dentist, who would, in a spotless holistic environment, pull a molar to drill out, clean up the rotting jaw bone. Doc's treatments included injecting Sanum Homeopathics into the gum, laser for cleaning out bacteria and infrared treatments post surgery. I felt this procedure to be worthy of having to apologize to my body for the severe invasion, but the clean out was necessary. After an 8:00 a.m. surgery, I'd be out by 12:00 noon to drive to the airport, catch a 2:30 plane, drive home, arriving just as the non-epinephrine anesthetic was leaving my face. Because of the ever present pressure in my head and my stance on pain meds which was, "I won't be able to know if I'm okay or not, plus I'm not interested in any drug-related side effects", I opted for taking 1M Arnica (Homeopathic remedy), some Vitamin C and using a hand held infrared lamp on my jaw bone. This was enough to get me through the pain. Sun on my face during the next few days was soothing.

At one appointment back in Santa Fe, my night guard needed more "material" added to it. I was naïve. The smell was nasty. I felt weird and was very soon embarrassed, apologizing for hitting the dentist because the apparatus had hurt as he placed it in my mouth. We were both surprised. He said, "No problem, people have done worse", but I learned that the smell of acrylic made me intolerant, angry, helpless, teary and aggressive. It had been a chemical sensitivity melt-down.

Along the way I did try crowns before having teeth pulled. I was insistent that they be porcelain, not wanting metal in my mouth. Having heavy metals and DDT exposure during childhood rendered me intolerant to metals, causing nerve pain. To my dismay, following a dental x-ray, I learned that a dentist had put in a porcelain crown with metal base. This metal touched the root, so I had to have it removed and replaced. I needed a clean mouth in hopes of reducing pain and pressure in my occipital area. The TMJ pain was ever *present and of course worse after each dental altering experience.*

During this time I was experimenting with Sensodyne toothpaste, tea tree oil, clove oil, peppermint oil, baking soda, diatomaceous earth, Vitamin D, Co Q-10, gum brushing, water picks, vibrating toothbrushes and special tooth oil combinations, all of which helped in some way, but also irritated my gums, my teeth and me.

Four and a half years after the accident, my Massage Therapist suggested I see an Osteopath, an hour away. I had absolutely NO hope, but went because she kept suggesting it.

Weekly, for two years, I traveled the 120 miles for the visits. The shoulder that had been fractured and frozen slowly became functional. (I had been swimming in the sulfur hot springs 3 to 5 times a week without using my arms.) This Osteopath would methodically begin at my feet, feeling the cranial rhythms, (or lack of) and after a year and a half the pressure in my head sparked out into his hands, enough to make him jump up from his seat. He was okay and I, much better.

With Skeletal Myofacial Massage and Cranial-sacral Osteopathy, the pronounced curves in my back began to relax and heal. The doctor worked for hours on my diaphragm, which had also been hurt in the wreck. He would kindly explain that we had to get the lower body stable before the neck, head and TMJ could be addressed. This was taking a long time because patterns had set in after the wreck, and they needed to be gently unwound. It would often take 24 hours before the exhaustion from the treatments dissipated.

Throughout this time I was primarily on a Vegan diet. I grew lots of dark greens. Some friends suggested I eat salmon. I tried salmon oil first but didn't feel much change. Eventually, I began eating "clean" salmon. I could feel my muscles strengthen, but my teeth and TMJ remained a nightmare.

Liquid colloidal magnesium would take the edge off of the pain at night, so I could sleep. I tried several types of calcium supplements including ionic liquid calcium which didn't seem to help. Trying yogurt, cow and goat, went against my alkaline diet, but I tried them. They clogged my lymph, even with lots of clove powder mixed in. Homeopathic silica didn't seem to help either.

Finally I found a calcium citrate powder. I dipped my toothbrush in liquid colloid calcium, then in the calcium powder, and finally found a way to brush my teeth with something that gave back to them. The sweetness in all the toothpastes had been too irritating.

In trying to heal the TMJ problem and the hurting teeth, I delved into emotional, psychological and spiritual introspection. I worked with Light and Sound Teachings, DVDs, books and tapes by Deepak Chopra, Carolyn Myss and anything at the library that dealt with forgiveness, the shadow and healing.

What I learned was that this pain would not be spiritually wished away. I had tried bargaining, promising, begging. What I could count on was Companionship for the work and the journey, not a free ride.

In my searching, I came across some exciting information. I didn't know if it was true but the energetics made sense. The author talked about a liquid, yes, a liquid in the teeth, in the dentin tubules. This liquid resembles the cerebral spinal fluid. It could move in two directions. It could bring bacteria into the teeth or nutrients from the body out to them. Immediately connecting with the impact of the car, I knew my energy was going from my mouth into my teeth. I had to change this in order to bring the nutrients from my bloodstream out into the teeth to make them healthier.

This, together with working with an Indigenous Healer, who worked at un-sticking the myelin sheath from the trigeminal nerve, and beginning healing treatments from the points of impact, in order to allow the trauma holding patterns to soften and clear, circulation began to increase. Working directly on the teeth roots (using a cranial-sacral approach) allowed the TMJ to stop hurting. (In part this was made possible because of all of the previous Osteopathic, self-help, massage and the plethora of other work which had created a foundation for healing.)

During these difficult times, acid food, especially fruit, hurt my teeth. Greens, raw and cooked, helped me feel stronger. Clean fish 4 to 8 times a month has been beneficial. Concentrating on bringing nutrients from inside me to my teeth has been a helpful change. Who would have thought to do this?

Perhaps you too are sensitive to local anesthetics? I would feel the negative effects for weeks. A local dentist told me that one of his patients would drink a liter of Coke before Novocaine. This helped her and I should try it. "No way," I thought! But if this helped someone there would have to be some truth to it.

Usually before a tooth extraction, I'd get alkaline but never ate. So, I tried something different. The night before, I ate some wild rice for its absorbing qualities. In the morning, fifteen minutes before the extraction, I drank 1/2 liter of carrot juice, figuring this would open up my cells to be more receptive, thinking that perhaps the cells would need less anesthetic? After the extraction, I took a 1 M of homeopathic Arnica. An hour later, I drank 1/2 liter of carrot juice, then after another hour, I drank 1 liter of a green drink (without spirulina or chlorella, which are algae). I relaxed in the hot springs for 1 1/2 hours. (You could take a warm Epsom salt bath.)

In the evening, a green vegetable potage soup was dinner with an herb tea. Guess what? I had hardly a trace of nerve discomfort or mind fog.

In talking with the dentist's patient, she told me that the Coke made in Mexico without corn syrup gave her liver a kick to detoxify the anesthetic.

What is in store for dentistry within the upcoming years? Crystal fillings, regrowing teeth roots using a tiny ultrasound frequency, tooth implants from stem cells, and regenerating our own stem cells to make a third set of teeth. Wow!

Back to the present, you may be wondering about root canals? Early on I was discouraged from having root canals because they leave a dead tooth in the bone which can cause deterioration of the bone, (according to My Dentist, Dr. Michael Margolis and the folks at Huggins, who do blood compatibility dentistry).

What can cause bone deterioration is pulling a tooth without cavitating the socket. Cavitation entails drilling with a burr 1 mm all around the extraction site to make sure that the attachment of the dental ligaments are not left in the bone. (Fragments of the dental ligaments can cause bone rot.)

Recently, I found a dentist in New Mexico that would do laser root canals. This meant he would clean out the nerve without anesthetics. I was tempted to try this. However when I thought it through, what I saw was that the nerve was hurting for a reason. If I removed it, it would be like removing fire alarms from my home. My pain would be gone but the cause of the pain would not be addressed and additional aberrations could ensue. Furthermore, I was unsure of the effects of the material used to fill the hole created by the nerve removal, so no root canal for me. Holistic dentists, in general, would concur.

This is a Summary of What has Been Helpful

1. Massaging my gums with my index finger or tongue
2. Applying essential oils to the gums or to the cheek if gum is too sensitive:
    - peppermint oil for pain
    - tea tree oil for infection
3. Packing the gums with:
    - turmeric (for infection and/or swelling)
    - myrrh powder (for infection and revitalization)
    - neem powder (for infection and/or swelling)
    - comfrey root (for soothing pain)
    - manjishta powder (to rebuild tissue)
    - gentian root (for swelling)
    - osha root (for pain and infection)
    - toothache plant (for pain)
4. Cleaning teeth after eating and drinking with Water Oz Iodine
5. Getting a blood compatibility test in order to use materials that are least offensive to the body (Bio Comp Lab: 800-331-2303)
6. Massage and Cranial-Sacral body work
7. Taking ionic magnesium before bed
8. Brushing teeth with Calcium Citrate powder
9. Eating 1 T. gelatin** daily. (1 T. gelatin gels 1 pint of liquid.) I called Knox Gelatin inquiring about the nutritive value of their gelatin. They told me that there wasn't any! Great Lakes makes a gelatin with an amino acid analysis on the label. Gelatin helps our bodies produce collagen for joint and bone health. I feel it is strengthening my gums and teeth. I make it with a green drink, fresh peppermint or sage tea or veggie broth. (**See Jello*.)

Pre and Post Dental Procedures

1. Drinking a lot of water and alkaline fluids to rid the body of anesthetics. (Bio Comp Labs told me that anesthetics leave the body within 3 days and that if we were not allergic to the anesthetic then it would not numb us!)

2. Taking homeopathic arnica before and after dental work. Homeopathic Hypericum can also be helpful

3. Taking Vitamin C for potential infections. açai powder has worked for me

4. If necessary, put a drop of tea tree oil on the infected gum

5. The best detoxifying liquid I have found is fresh wheat grass juice. You can make this in a blender with 1/2 quart of water, adding some fresh mint

6. Geranium essential oil on the liver and on the liver point on the foot where you can feel the "V" between the big toe and the next toe has been helpful for detox.

During the Dental Work

1. Quietly blessing the dentist and helpers

2. Being thankful that I would be receiving the best help possible from earthly beings and Spirit

3. Opting at first for Carbocaine rather than Novocain (which contains epinephrine which can speed up the heart causing discomfort). Septocaine in minute amounts around the tooth seems to be even better for upper dental work, (since it does not contain carcinogens, although it does contain epinephrine)

4. When possible, having Septocaine injected all around the tooth to be worked on rather than into the nerves near the mandible and TMJ. Septocaine can cause paralysis if used as a lower jaw nerve block

5. Making sure that the crown (even porcelain crowns, unbeknown to dentists, can be made of 40% aluminum, according to Dr. Huggins) are aluminum free. Bio Comp Lab says that all porcelain teeth contain aluminum

6. If an amalgam filling was changed out, a rubber dam was used to catch the pieces of filling that I could have swallowed. Ingesting or breathing even particles of amalgams can be detrimental to our livers and immune systems

7. Getting Skeletal Myofacial Massage, Cranial work, and Osteopathy has been invaluable

8. Adapting my normal 80:20 alkaline diet to include higher amounts of specific mineral foods.

Recipe for Healthy Teeth

You can research the following information then write your own recipe after you have cautiously tested each ingredient. For example, because my body responds to 1/4 the dose usually recommended for herbs, that's where I begin.

As you will discover, different nutritional sources give varying information. We don't have consistent air or water quality, earth components, weather or human energy put into food and herbs. At best, we are offered an approximation of the nutrients we eat (which is different from what we absorb).

Sometimes herb contents are specific, however many times we are told that an herb, for instance contains iron. It is difficult, as in the case of yellow dock, to find exactly how much. So we have to pay attention. We need to know our bodies and be able to tell the difference between something hurting us or causing a healing crisis and what nourishes us. The bottom line is that we are the responsible ones for our health. It takes courage to seek the advice of others, then to sift through the information to apply what we are willing to stand accountable for. I applaud you who are willing to, as Carolyn Myss says, "Move from being a noun to a verb."

Getting more specific with my alkaline diet I needed to include the following, keeping in mind other nutritional needs, such as caloric intake.

Calcium, Phosphorus (for healthy dentin), Vitamins A, D, and fat are nutrients which are important to get from foods, not supplements.

Minimum Daily Requirements for Healthy Teeth
(For middle-age adults)

Calcium – 1200 mg (milligrams)
Phosphorus – 500 to 800 mg
Vitamin A – 800 IU (international units)
Vitamin D – 400 IU

To heal damage, as a guideline, increase these to:

Calcium – 1500 mg
Phosphorus – 2000 mg
Vitamin A – 10,000 IU
Vitamin D – 1,000 IU
Manganese – 1.5 mg
Fat

According to Dr. Melvin Price we also need to pay attention to the calcium/phosphorous ratio. The ratio for healthy teeth is 2 1/2 parts calcium to 1 part phosphorous, or else the dentin begins to lose minerals. For teeth which have been de-mineralized and are deteriorating, more phosphorous is recommended.

The following is a list of foods which enabled me to see just what I needed to eat to help heal my mouth. There were two powerhouse foods, amaranth and seeds. These foods enabled me to stay close to an alkaline lifestyle.

Calcium Sources 1200-1500 mg per day	mg
1 C. acorn squash	240
1/4 C. almonds	235
1 C. amaranth	535
1 C. beans	100
1 C. bok choy (steamed)	158
1 C. broccoli (steamed)	95
2 T. chia seeds	177
1 T, cinnamon	84
1 C. collards (steamed)	226
1 T. dill seeds	100
5 figs	135
1 T. flax seed	57
1/2 C. kale (steamed)	250
1 T. molasses	172
1 T. oregano	85
1 T. poppy seeds	125
1 C. quinoa	100
4 oz salmon (with bones)	200
1 T. sesame seeds	165
1 C. spinach (steamed)	140
20-30 minutes of sunshine daily adds in calcium absorption	

Phosphorous Sources 500-12000 mg per day	mg
1 C. adzuki beans	386
1/2 C. almonds	350
1 C. amaranth	887
1 C. barley	485
1 cup beans	296
1 C. brazil nuts	435
1 C. buckwheat	523
5 figs	54
1 C. garbanzo beans	276
1 C. lentils	376
1 C. millet	570
1 C. parsnips	108
2 T, pumpkin seeds	338
1 C. quinoa	697
1/4 C. sesame seed	222
1/4 C. sunflower seed	303
3 oz. trout	256
1 C. wild rice	692

I am not a huge fan of soy as it is high in phytic acid which blocks the absorption of calcium, magnesium, copper, iron and zinc in the small intestines. When trying to heal my teeth, soy seemed counterproductive.

Vitamin A Sources 800 IU - 10,000 IU per day	IU
1 C. cantaloupe	5400
1 raw carrots	8600
1/2 C. steamed carrots	13410
1/2 C. steamed kale	9550
1 C. fresh mango	1260
1 C. fresh papaya	1500
1/2 C. frozen peas	1050
1 C. raw spinach	2800
1/2 C. steamed spinach	11458

Vitamin D Sources 400 IU - 1000 IU per day	IU
1 T. cod liver oil (unrefined)	5400
3 1/2 oz. cooked salmon	13410
1 glass of milk	1260

Remember that we get Vitamin D from the skin's response to the sun. Dark skinned individuals need 20% to 30% more sun than fair skins. Time of year and latitude need to be factored in. For instance, people who live longitudinally north of Massachusetts probably need to supplement during the winter.

Elderly people need more sunlight because it's more difficult for them to make the Vitamin D. If we have white skin and it turns pink during a sunbath, we are making about 10,000-20,000 I.U. of Vitamin D.

Next, magnesium, copper, iron and manganese are needed for a healthy flow of the fluid through the dentin, says Dr. Price.

Magnesium Sources 320 mg per day	mg
1/4 C. almonds	98
1 C. black beans	120
1 C. buckwheat	85
2 T. flax seed	70
1 C. cooked collards	32
1 C. millet	105
1 C. quinoa	89
4 oz. cooked salmon	138

Copper Sources 900 mg per day	mg
1 C. avocado	235
1 C. barley	270
! C. steamed beets	74
2 T. flax seed	95
1 C. garbanzo beans	270
1 C. lentils	229
1 C. navy beans	250
1/4 C. pumpkin seeks	186
1/4 C. sesame seeds	206
1/4 C. sunflower seeds	205

Iron Sources 18 mg per day for women under 50 10 mg per day for men and women over 50	mg
1 T. anise seed	2.45
4 whole dried apricots	2.5
1 C. beet greens**	2.7
1 C. black eyed peas	4.3
1 T. cumin	3.9
1/2 C. dates	2.5
1 C. broccoli	1.0
1 T. fenugreek	3.72
5 dried figs	2.0
1/2 C. dark leafy greens-cooked	2.0
1 C. green beans	1.0
1 C. kale	1.2
1 C. lentils	6.0
1 C. lima beans	6.4
1 C. millet	1.5
1 T. molasses	3.5
1 T. dried parsley	1.95
2 T. pumpkin seeds	2.5
1/2 C. raisins	1.5
2 T. dried rosemary	2.0
1/4 T. sesame seeds	2.8
1 C. raw spinach**	1.0
1 C. cooked spinach**	6.5
1 C. cooked swiss chard**	2.0
1/4 C. sunflower seeds	8.0
2 T. dried thyme	7.4
1 C. tofu	13.0
1 T. turmeric	2.8

**Iron absorption is enhanced with Vitamin C.

The minimum daily requirement for iron is measured by the elemental iron. Iron can also be regarded as heme or non-heme iron. The iron in animal foods is called heme and is easily absorbed. Plant matter is non-heme and is said to be less readily absorbed by the body. In addition, many plants contain oxalic acid. This inhibits the absorption of iron. Plants that contain oxalic acids are many of the dark green leafy vegetables, for example: beet greens, Swiss chard, and spinach. Other plants which contain oxalic acid are whole grains, sweet potatoes, rhubarb, soy, coffee, tea and red wine. This does not mean that these foods should be avoided. Eating them with a source of Vitamin C will release the iron and make it available for absorption; simply add fresh lemon juice, bell peppers or fresh tomatoes to your meal.

It seems that dried herbs contain more iron than fresh herbs, and cooking greens generally increases the amount of iron in food. Cooking in cast iron pans also increases the iron content in food. If the pan has not been seasoned, more iron goes into the food. Although I've found no information that cooking in cast iron is harmful, I prefer getting iron from living sources. Whether the iron is heme or non-heme, we still only absorb a very small percentage. What spurred me into exploring iron was that I was tired…not sleepy and I had bone pain in my jaw and face. What I learned was that when we are low on iron and want to boost it, never to go over 45 mg per day because too much iron may cause other major problems; 200 mg. can be lethal.

In addition, there are foods which inhibit or interfere with calcium absorption; alcohol, smoking (which also robs the body of Vitamin C which is necessary in the production of collagen), caffeine in large amounts, peanuts, soybeans, too much or too little protein, large amounts of fat, salt and sugars, phosphorous containing drinks like soda, and lack of exercise or movement.

The information on carbonated water is conflicting. It makes sense to drink carbonated water from a glass bottle with some fresh lemon or lime juice or ginger tea, rather than soda pop, but the information is not yet clear if the carbonation is a leaching factor for calcium.

The best one can do is to test the pH of carbonated water, choosing the highest pH, and then muscle test to see if you test positive or negative for it. Choose high pH water for an alkaline diet. Then observe if the hurting parts feel better or worse and see if the healthy parts feel inhibited or energized.

Manganese Sources 1.8 mg per day	mg
1 C. steamed beets	.55
1 C. steamed broccoli	.34
1 C. buckwheat	.68
1 C. collard greens (steamed)	1.07
2 T. flax seed	.64
1 C. garbanzo beans	1.7
1 C. lentils	.49
1 C. cooked millet	.66
1 C. peas	.84

Manganese Sources 1.8 mg per day	mg
1/4 C. pumpkin seeds	1.04
1/2 C. quinoa	.96
1 C. raspberries	1.24
2 C. romaine lettuce	.71
1 C. brown rice	1.76
1/4 C. sesame seed	.88
1 C. steamed spinach	1.68
1/4 C. sunflower seeds	.88
1/4 C. walnuts	.85

The dentin tubules contain a fluid where nutrients can flow from the body to the teeth to fortify them. Ramiel Nagel, a student of Dr. Price, says that teeth can be re-mineralized to make new enamel. The specific diet that these two men have developed has nothing to do with cholesterol, calories, heart health or acid-alkalinity.

Dr. Price advises eating fat, butter (1/2 Tbs. three times daily) from cows who eat rapidly growing summer wheat or rye grass (not grains). Cows eating these grasses are able to convert Vitamin K1 to Vitamin K2. The resulting butter contains the necessary vitamin factors that help bond mineral to bone. This high vitamin butter is, according to Dr. Price, the missing link to tooth decay reversal because it builds hydroxyapatite, a calcium phosphate ceramic that is used as a biomaterial, which helps prevent tooth decay. They do not advise taking hydoxyapatite in pill form.

The Price diet also includes raw meat, honey, coconut oil, avocado, olive oil, bone marrow, oysters, organ meats, bone broth, fish eggs, fish head soups, fermented cod liver oil, and raw milk products such as butter, kefir, cream, cheese and yogurt.

Here is a sample alkaline meal plan which includes the higher amounts of minerals:

	Calcium 1,500 mg,	Phosphorous 2,000 mg.	Vitamin A 10,000 I.U.	Vitamin D 1,000 I.U.
Breakfast				
1 C. amaranth	535 mg	885 mg		
1/4 C. soaked almonds	125 mg	175 mg		
1 T. ground cinnamon	85 mg			
Freshly made green drink				
Lunch:				
Green salad with 1/2 cup arugula	63 mg			
1 T. ground chia seeds	177 mg			
1 large carrot			11,000 IU	
1 C. quinoa	100 mg	690 mg		
Snack:				
1/4 C. soaked sunflower seeds Outside in the sun		300 mg		outside in the sun
Supper:				
4 oz. salmon	250 mg			360 IU
1 C. steamed collards	210 mg			
Mixed salad with peppers with 2 T. ground sesame seeds olive oil, and lemon	300 mg	110 mg		

The Huggins System and Quantum Dental Health System

To conclude, allow me to summarize what the two leading edge dental systems use in their practices.

The Huggins system (started by Dr. Huggins) is extremely careful about removing silver amalgam fillings. Dr. Huggins' research has led him to link M.S. and female breast cancer with these fillings. Special protocols are used, which include digital x-rays, a device to see how much electromagnetic toxicity teeth are giving off along with meticulously removing amalgams so that the patient doesn't breathe or swallow any particles which are being removed. Oftentimes oxygen is administered along with the use of a rubber dam and high suction. They are proponents of bio-compatible materials. Bio-compatibility is achieved through a blood test to suggest the least toxic materials for the patient.

If a tooth needs to be extracted, the bone is cavitated, drilled with a burr, 1mm to insure that all of the periodontal ligaments are removed. Some dentists will then use a laser to clean out any possible bacteria.

Strict "Huggins" dentists do not use animal or synthetic material to add to the bone's structure before sewing up the cavitated area In the procedure room they will have a high tech air purifier.

Materials for crowns, bridges, dentures and partials vary according to the patient's immune system.

The second leading edge dental system is called the Quantum Dental Health System. It is the protocol that Dr. Randolf Aguilere and Dr. Robert Marshall have created.

These doctors do not use blood bio-compatibility. They use a limited number of products which they say are non-toxic.

They say that digital x-rays emit 90% less radiation. Apparently Novocain, Lidocaine and Carbocaine (which is an anesthetic without epinephrine, for those who'd prefer not experiencing a racing heart) are made with aniline homologs which are carcinogenic, (meaning carcinogens are injected into the gums!) The Quantum Health dentists use Septocaine, which has 2% to 4% epinephrine and is said to be non-carcinogenic.

However, what I've read says that no cancer tests have been performed on Septocaine. One of the side effects can be paralysis if used as a nerve block on the lower jaw. In addition there are other dentists that recommend intravenous Demerol as an alternative.

These Quantum dentists use a detector to show micro fractures which don't show up on x-rays.

They also use a dental wand which administers the oral anesthetic drop by drop. This is important, so that the patient doesn't have to experience the normal pain experienced with getting numbed up.

Neither of these two leading edge dental systems use water laser drills. Information on water lasers repeatedly says that little or no anesthetic is needed and that water lasers keep the tooth from getting too hot.

Quantum Health dentists claim that the materials they use are non-toxic. From what I have read and experienced, there is no such thing as non-toxic dental materials. However, some seem to be less toxic, and I recommend personally researching every item, as some didn't seem to have extensive testing.

Dental Materials: The Best Choices
Recommended Biocompatible Dental Materials

Please remember—every dental material that is used in your mouth is of *critical* importance and must be carefully chosen. You (and your immune system) will be exposed to these dental materials 24/7 nonstop—continuously via your mouth. If a material tests even slightly poorly, it can negatively impact your body's health over time.

Note: Identifying nontoxic bonding agents is equally important as dental restoratives.

Although the following list appears very small, very few materials are able to meet our minimum standards for truly biocompatible dental materials which do not impede ideal cellular resonance for human beings. The following materials do not need to be allergy-tested because they are nontoxic. We have thoroughly tested them to be sure they do not impede the cellular resonance of the human body.

Note: Certain dental materials may test toxic in their "wet" or pre-formed state, but once they have hardened (and out-gassed) they may then test okay. Therefore, testing dental materials must be done in their final state.

After testing hundreds of people over many years, we have found the following dental materials have proven to be reliably biocompatible for most people and are all part of the **Quantum Dental Health System** (as taught by Dr. Marshall and Dr. Aguilera). These materials are used in the dental offices of Dr. Randy Aguilera in Austin, TX and in Orange County, CA. (To contact his office for further details, call: 888-793-7339.)

For Onlays, Inlays, Crowns

1. **Ceramics and Resin Ceramic Hybrids**

   Luminesse Ceramic (LFC–low-fusing ceramic)

   Vitablock (LFC; milled on Cerec milling unit, a chairside dental CAD/CAM restorative system

   MZ100 (LFC ceramic/resin hybrid – needed when extensive toot structure is missing; milled on Cerec milling unit)

   Cristobal+ (ceramic/resin hybrid)

   Degussa Ceramic (LFC; its trade name is Ducera Gold – a confusing name since it contains no gold.)

2. **Composites**

   Esthet-X

For Bridges

Solidex with Ribbond (ceramic/resin hybrid)

Cristbal+ with Robbond (ceramic/resin hybrid)

Cercon (ceramic)

For Dentures

(Avoid pink dyes in the denture base material which typically contain cadmium, a toxic metal.)

Dentsply Lucitone 199 (for base material of denture)

Valplast (for unilateral partials or full dentures

For Implants

We firmly recommend against using titanium implants which can create significant metallic and electrical distress.

We are currently investigating the best implants (for missing teeth); we are especially looking at low-fusing ceramic dental implants which are biocompatible with the human body.

Dental Bonding System (Needed for use with ceramic restorations or composites as listed above)

Se Clearfil (A strong bonding system)

Rely X ARC (Do not use its accompanying etch, prime and bond; use Se Clearfil)

Rely X-Unicem (Has a slightly stronger bond; contains all four agents together: etch, prime, bond, adhesive; do not need Se Clearfil)

Disinfection Methods (Needed before bonding dental materials to the tooth structure)

Research shows that the use of hydrogen peroxide (typcially used in dentistry) is *not* adequate—yielding only about 40% disinfection at best. For disinfection after dental procedures, we recommend that you go to a dentist who uses dental lasers (there are 3 key types of dental lasers: Diode, Nd-Yag, Erbium) which yield 99.9% disinfection

I apologize for offering you some dental hope. Yes, the nutrition portion can be helpful, but if you check on the web what dental products are causing Neuro-Cutaneous Syndrome you will see that Dr. Amin has come up with a list of over 350 dental materials which are toxic. (This list includes the ones that have been said to be non-toxic.) So the blood compatibility testing says it like it is: testing to see which dental chemicals will be the least toxic.

There is a researcher in Canada who is working on a bile filling. The bile portion is hopefully non-toxic, but it still needs to go through all the testing.

So, for those who still have healthy teeth, it's really important to eat to fortify them. For those with teeth problems, do try a nutritional approach, if you can, before introducing dental toxins to your body. Who knows the gamut effect of these chemicals on our immune systems?

Let's end this section on a note of hope. Here in the U.S., Dr. Julian Shu has mixed bile salts with chemical fillers to form a resin that hardens enough to be used as potential fillings. (We'll have to see if all the fillers can create a non-toxic alternative to today's fillings.) In France 'research' has come up with a gel that is put on carries. It cleans out the decay without the use of a drill and repairs the tooth! These products are years away for us consumers, but here's to hope and progress!

Additional Information

The following is my latest dental experience which may be helpful to some.

Dominique, now living in Encinitas, Ca came across a flyer at the Ace hardware store which gave information about the "Huggins" Bio Dental Center in Tijuana, Mexico. This office is located in the Grand Hotel which hosts several other healing modalities, (i.e. hyperbaric oxygen chambers). This group of dentists received further training in Huggins protocol.

The initial phone conversation was positive…a non metal partial could be made with Lucitone at 1/2 the normal price. Packing up my car, I arrived after a beautiful and long ride, to Encinitas where Dominique and my mother live. Dominique offered to "accompany" me.

I was still in culture shock, having been use to driving 25 m.p.h. through our 1 main street in Pagosa, to 5 lanes, each way buzzing at 70 m.p.h. But this did not give me a clue as to the additional shock of crossing the border into Mexico. I am writing this to give you the preparation I would have appreciated.

The U.S. has various scents. Tijuana has delicious cooking veggies smells… and sewer smells. The curbs are dirty and broken. The traffic is bedlam. Walking on the street was a constant verbal experience by hawkers, saying things like, "Ladies, come into my store. Come in and let me sell you something that you don't need!" The cabs don't have meters. There are only one or two lines that are reputed to be safe enough to enter. Dominique was no longer "accompanying" me. She was guiding and guarding. I am glad that her Marine training is still being of use today. Before getting into a cab, she would ask the price, then tell them she had gone there before for 1/2 the price, and they would say o.k. She was prepared with a detailed map of the city which she would comment on if we diverted from the prescribed route.

I was able to relax for a nano second, first getting into the cab, only to realize during take-off that the entire cab rattled, that there didn't seem to be driving protocol or politeness or speed limits. Every cab we took sounded and felt like it was losing parts. It usually cost $5 to get to the Grand Hotel and always cost more to return!

Entering Mexico was easy. We'd park in a lot or on the street, walked for about 10 minutes then went through a metal turnstile. Everyone and everything was welcoming in Mexico. Returning was different. Often, people would wait 2 hours in line to get through two inspections. On the third night the line was longer than a mile, so Dominique said, "Let's pay."

She haggled with the 'guy' hawking alongside the pedestrian line, agreeing to pay $5 for each of us, to walk us up to the front of the line, and to shove us into our new position, hoping we wouldn't be butted out. I was not looking forward to this experience, so I was thrilled when instead, without warning she hoped onto a small bus.

The bus started leaving before I knew what to do, so the "guy" behind me started yelling at the driver, who let me on. Then the "guy" was yelling at me! because he wanted his money, and I thought the $ would now be for the bus driver! Dominique motioned to pay him, as the bus moved on…only a few meters, for our 1/2 hour wait. I asked the man next to me what kind of a bus this was, public or free? He said it was a "special" bus with a "special" number! I asked how the bus driver got paid. "The man who got you on the bus gives the driver a cut of what you gave him." I shut up. After the INS escorted us to a line in immigration, the bus was totally inspected, under the hood, included.

Here are some going-through-immigration unspoken but useful guidelines. Remove sunglasses, look at the officer straight in the eye, answer interrogation questions with one or two words, have your passport open so it can easily be swiped, and don't bother smiling! Some of my questions were, "What did you *buy in Mexico, what are you bringing back, what were you doing there, what is your last name?"* I needed to show another form of i.d. to show I have only 1 name. Then all bags pass through x-ray, don't look back…keep walking until you are beyond the orange plastic cones, outside the exit.

For this portion of the dental trip, I'd recommend going with a friend, preferably one who has experience in Tijuana. Bring lots of singles ($) so no change has to be made, sunglasses, a hat for the sun and heat, a jacket for when the sun goes down. Drink only bottled water and beverages, eat only packaged and well cooked food, and forget about time. Take a hot bath or shower in the evening and rub your hands and feet with tea tree oil at the end of the day. My mother, who was 88 years old, has participated in this dental adventure, accompanied by my sister, so it is possible for most of us. Simply expect a different way of everything in Tijuana, and you'll be fine.

Now for the actual dental experience: The Grand Hotel with its high twin towers shakes. No one knows why!

Sauntering about the reception area of the 3 stall and one surgical room office was an elegant, relaxed, smiling bilingual man. The receptionist called me by name as I walked in the front door! Dominique was offered a free exam, so we both filled out a simple intake form which included, "Is there something that you would like to share with the dentist in private?"

I went first, making the comment to the young man in baggy jeans, who examined my teeth that I was looking forward to meeting the dentist. He replied, "I am the dentist! Would you like to talk with Alex? He is an older man?" Honestly, I couldn't believe this young man was old enough to be a dentist. And I did speak with Alex, the sauntering CEO who affirmed that he'd had lots of trouble with Dr. Diaz when he first arrived 6 years ago, because at 25 he looked 17!

Mr. A. Porcella explained in great detail the results, protocol for treatment, and prices for follow-up. I agreed to have impressions made and was told to return in 1/2 hour for the second part of the impressions. An hour later wax impressions were made. We made appointments to have Dominique's amalgams changed out.

Five days later we returned. The partials had to be remade because they were pink, not clear. (Remember? pink = cadmium) Dominique had one side, upper and lower amalgams changed out, complete with a vitamin C I.V. Dominique has a Doctorate in Physical Therapy. She is precise. After her visit her mouth was soar but concurred that Dr. Diaz was gentle and she was happy with his work.

Our third appointment was for the teeth on the other side of her mouth and to fit my partials. When Dr. Diaz looked at my bite with the clear Lucitone partials in place, he said, "terrible, this is terrible," and for the next hour he whittled the partials so that my bite was comfortable.

He told me that most people usually need another adjustment and to come back if I did.

I did need another adjustment, but didn't want to deal with the immigration line for a fourth time. I was happy with the Lucitone partials, and would borrow Dominique's Dremmel to make further adjustments to the partials.

Two months after getting the new partials I arrived in Phoenix to deal with a tooth that had been painful for nine months when exposed to liquids or pressure. The x-rays showed no problems with the tooth. My Dentist filed down the tooth and covered it with a liquid sealer. We gave it a month to calm down. It did but the core was still painful. Doc did some muscle testing and we decided to extract it. It wouldn't get numb. I said, "Just pull it." In two seconds it was out! Doc cavitated the area and I asked about the condition of the root. He said that the tooth was fine but that the socket was cracked in 3 places! Now the bone would fill in. The tooth had parts of the ligaments attached to it. It was obvious that some of the attachments had not come out with the tooth, so I was fortunate to be with a dentist that would remove the pieces left in the jawbone.

For this extraction, I made different preparations. Instead of drinking liquids, I ate some lentils and took some milk thistle to get the liver ready for detoxing the anesthetic. I took some liquid iodine beforehand to fill the receptors to minimize radiation effects, in case an x-ray was required. Post surgery I drank a green drink (cucumber, parsley, kale and celery), and later ate some Indian Basmati rice for its absorbing qualities. 1 M Arnica (homeopathic pellet) was all I needed for pain, along with 2 white willow bark capsules for swelling. This left me as though I hardly felt that I had been to the dentist.

The mystery of the "perfect" tooth was now solved and I was happy. The following week I learned about StemSave, a group in Phoenix that collects and saves extracted teeth for their stem cells. I think this is a good investment for wonderful possibilities in the future.

P.S. Here is a later adventure which may be helpful to you.

I was in the hot springs here in Pagosa. Alex asked me "como estas?" I said, "mi dente hurts." He sauntered over and asked, "Have you tried putting rattlesnake powder on it?" I said, "WHAT?" Alex calmly replied, "Rattlesnake powder will take the pain away." "Alex, where would I get rattlesnake powder?" "Zeena," as he calls me, "You don't have any?" "No, Alex, I don't and where would one get some?" "I might have some in storage. Let me check." "Alex, where did you learn about rattlesnake powder?" "My mother used to give it to us every morning when we were children." "Why Alex?" "She said it would keep us healthy."

For a second opinion, I went to see my car mechanic and said. "Eddie, do you have any rattlesnake powder?" "What for?" "I have a toothache." "Did you take Osha?" "Yes, but it didn't help." "Well then, the powder will." "Do you have any?" "No, but I will check around." I left with a hopeful heart.

Two days later, there was a message on my phone machine to come down to a local restaurant. There, I was escorted into the kitchen where the cook said, "What do you want it for?" "I have a toothache." He told me that he didn't have any but he'd look around. Two days later I was instructed to come down to the restaurant.

The cook was too busy to see me, but a waitress handed me a baggie with powder in it. I asked what I owed. She shrugged her shoulders. I gave her a bag of Southwest almonds I had roasted. She smiled and we parted.

Back at the pool, I asked Alex what I should do with it. "Make a ball with Vicks, put the powder in it and put it on your tooth." "What? Eat Vicks?" "That's how we do it." Well, I couldn't, but I did put some on a cotton ball and kept it in my mouth (changing it every few hours) for 24 hours. Did I get pain relief? Yes. Did it taste disgusting? Yes. Was I spitting out the bones as Alex had intimated? Yes.

Alex explained that the powder was made from the front and back six inch ends of the snake and that the bones were included in the powder.

Online, I found rattlesnake pills available in Mexico (in case my small baggie ran out). There were some problems with these pills: salmonella and e-coli!

Several times I used this rattlesnake powder compress. It took some time to feel relief, but I did. I figured that the reason that the powder was helpful was that the calcium from the bones and who knows what from the snake was providing my gums, jawbone and teeth something it needed.

So I tried two more things. I asked a dentist to coat the biting areas of the two bottom front teeth. He called it a green and red filling. This involved spraying the teeth with air which contained diamond dust. After the filling liquid was painted on, it was baked. It was painless and I felt good to have added protection.

Not wanting to rely on rattlesnake powder, I looked at ways to supplement calcium, feeling that my body needed more or a different form. I tried all the calcium supplements that didn't have silicon dioxide or ascorbic acid. None felt good, including calcium citrate powder and calcium phosphate, which is best for nourishing teeth. Then I tried yogurt, plain cow, sheep, goat, full fat, two percent, non-fat, in glass containers, lactose free, all of which stuffed my nose and lymphatics. Finally, Sonne's liquid calcium was easily digestible. In addition, rinsing my mouth with Water Oz Liquid Iodine made sure that my mouth stayed clear on unwanted pathogens. (There are other forms of iodine, but they are either made from kelp, which may no longer be clean, or the liquid usually contains alcohol which would not be healthy.)

Perhaps sharing this dental journey has been helpful for you? My hope is that this information will help prevent dental problems for our children and assist adults with existing oral challenges. May you be Guided.

In closing, I appreciate your interest in wanting to become healthier. Any step towards eating locally, eating live unadulterated foods, paying attention to moving from an acid diet to an alkaline life style helps you and all of us. Thank you for your time and efforts. May you continue to grow in vibrancy.

Zhéna

About the Author

Zhéna has been helping people to eat according to their particular needs for the past 35 years.

Her background includes working with the Standard American diet, French, Macrobiotic, Ayurvedic, and Alkaline cooking.

In the '70s she was the chef/owner of Zhéna's Cuisine, a fine vegetarian restaurant in Amherst, Mass.

To order this book, and for nutritional and microscopy consultations email Zhéna at alkalinecuisine.net

CPSIA information can be obtained at www.ICGtesting.com
Printed in the USA
BVOW052355021212
307025BV00002B/6/P